D1370634

FISH Schtick

A simple humorous guide to the secrets of fish and seafood.

John Wood
with Christopher McNulty

Doubleday Canada Limited

Preface

$\mathcal{C}$ ongratulations, you did it! Regardless of whether you bought, borrowed or stole this book, you've just taken the first step in learning more about fish.

When "Baldrick" (who still isn't sure about any kind of book learning) and I (who pretend to know something about it) decided to write this masterpiece, we weren't sure if the world really needed another cookbook. However, after talking to friends and relatives, we put our heads together and decided there was indeed a need to share our knowledge of purchasing and preparing fish. Fish and their relatives still remain a mystery to much of the general public. At a time when people are becoming more and more health-conscious and are choosing a healthier lifestyle, fish has become a nutritious alternative to red meat. But the only way that most people buy it is between two buns and in a styrofoam container from a fast food chain. We want to help you break this habit and make fish a welcome part of your everyday cooking.

We also want to make it simple for you to do this. Most seafood cookbooks try to build a mystique around the art of cooking fish. If you're not daunted by the complicated cooking methods, you will be by the hunt for obscure ingredients, found only in remote parts of the globe. The next hurdle is then to mortgage your house in order to pay for them.

Last, but not least, we have seven daughters between us to feed, clothe and educate. Therefore, we are willing to offer our combined knowledge of "fish facts" in return for your generous donations and support.

This book is intended to be light, informative and with a little humor thrown in to show you how easy it is to enjoy your favorite fish at home as well as with us. You will note as you flip through these pages that we have included tips for buying and cleaning fish, as well as popular recipes. We also felt it was important to provide you with some information on the origin of certain fish, how they are prepared and some of the experiences we have had with them. Let's face it, any restaurant calling itself the "Old Fish Market" must have some very fishy tales to tell.

If you bought this book, thank you. If you stole it, shame on you. If you borrowed it, please return it to its original owner — obviously he or she has excellent taste. However, if you're just thumbing through this copy at your local bookstore and have no intention of purchasing it, put it down immediately. Information gained thus far has cost you thirty-seven cents, so pay up on your way out.

Old Fish Market Restaurants

The Old Fish Market Restaurants started operation in 1975 opposite the St. Lawrence Market, which was Toronto's original municipal fish market. Situated on the waterfront, the earliest building on the site was a frame hotel. In 1910, a brick hotel was erected to replace the wooden structure and operated until 1917. It was far from being a grand hotel; excellent beverages and location seemed to be the determining factor in attracting its clientele of sailors and fishermen. The hotel also provided a local meeting place for businessmen involved in market dealings.

The initial address of the hotel was West Market Square; however, in 1919 the name was changed to Market Street. To make things even more confusing, Wellington Street West was known as Market Street until 1840. As the street name changed over the years, so too did the name of the hotel — The Heaslips Hotel, Millsgate Hotel, Armory Hotel, Old Armory Hotel and the New Market Hotel. Across the street from the hotel, the St. Lawrence Hall (now the St. Lawrence Market) was used over the years as the town hall, the city jail and the armory.

In 1917, the hotel became a wholesale leather and hides store; then it was turned into the Market Garage in 1933 and the St. Lawrence Garage in 1940. In 1975, it was an auto accessory shop before becoming the Old Fish Market Restaurant. By this time, land that had been previously owned by the government was reclaimed for industry, and the building was no longer positioned on the waterfront. The view of Lake Ontario had become virtually lost.

In 1984, the present structure was listed as a historical building and, as in bygone days, the Old Fish Market Restaurant continues to invite people from all parts of the world to come and enjoy food and beverages. Our Windsor and Ottawa locations are also situated close to fresh food markets, allowing us to keep our promise of providing tantalizing food, a pleasant atmosphere and affordable prices. We have received many awards, notably the Neptune Award from the Canadian Seafood Council. The menu is changed twice daily in an effort to offer our patrons the freshest selection of seafood. Our fish is cooked and served the only way it should be: simply and precisely. Sauces are kept to a minimum to prevent the masking of delicate flavors. We want you to savor the taste of every mouthful.

Although we own a number of other restaurants, ranging from wine bars to pool rooms, our first love will always be the Old Fish Market.

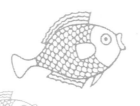

$\mathcal{L}$earning about Fish

$\mathcal{A}$s three-quarters of the earth is covered by water, it's fair to assume that there are a wide variety of fishy things living beneath the waves. There are literally hundreds and hundreds of different species, far too many to mention in this book. What we will do is divide the fish into four groups: saltwater, freshwater, fat and lean.

Saltwater Fish: In this group can be found both round and flat fish. Some examples of the most common round fish from the sea are cod, haddock, whiting, pollock and orange roughy. Some of the most common examples of flat fish are halibut, sole, flounder and turbot.

Freshwater Fish: These fish are found in lakes and rivers, and are either caught and farmed commercially or are caught by the authors and their daughters, who love to fish. In the salmon family are arctic char, lake trout, whitefish, brook trout, brown trout and, of course, the different varieties of salmon, including sockeye, coho, chum and chinook. Other freshwater fish include pickerel, northern pike or walleye, mullet, goldeye and yellow perch.

Fat or Oily Fish: This group comprises only round fish and includes herring and mackerel. Five percent of the body weight of these fish is fat. Fish from the freshwater category are also found in this group, especially if purchased in late summer and fall when they are building up fat supplies to see them through the winter. Two good examples of this type of fish are whitefish and lake trout.

Lean Fish: This group is almost identical to the fish from the sea group except that all the fish in it contain less than 5 percent fat. Found in this group are monkfish, grouper, ocean perch and members of the sole family.

At this time, we should make the point that there is nothing wrong in eating an oily or fat fish. If eaten in moderation, it can be part of a well-balanced diet. One can lessen the fat content in meals using these types of fish simply by choosing to grill or steam the fish instead of the more popular method of deep-frying. Go ahead, be creative: you'll be pleasantly surprised when you try new and delicious ways to cook fish.

Helpful Hints about Purchasing Fish

A common assumption about fish is that fresh is always best. But is it? What does "fresh" really mean? In most cases it means that the product has been caught, gutted and kept on ice while still at sea. However, most fish sit on the deck of a boat for a few days after being caught, then they are cleaned, chilled and shipped to your local fish purveyor on ice. Or does "fresh" mean that the product is caught, gutted, cleaned, blast frozen and stored in a perfect condition at sea and then shipped in this state to the consumer?

Obviously, there are two definitions of "fresh." Many restaurants and fish markets boast that their fish is fresh. What that means is that it has never been frozen. It could have been chilled and washed in a salt solution for seven days, though. Thus, your best bet is to use a supplier who has a good reputation, is knowledgeable about fish and doesn't make wild claims concerning the freshness of his fish. It's up to you to decide whether you want to serve the fish you buy that same evening or store it frozen for use at a later date. We leave you with the words *caveat emptor* ("let the buyer beware"). That's about all the Latin we know and all the Latin you'll need to get through this book.

Buying Fresh Fish

When purchasing non-frozen fish, here are a few simple rules to follow to ensure its freshness:

§ If fish is whole — rainbow trout or red snapper, for example — look for bright and full, not sunken, eyes.

§ Fish gills should be bright and clean.

§ If the fish has scales, they should be plentiful and there should be no bald patches.

§ In all fish, the flesh should be firm and there should be no unpleasant smells.

Buying Frozen Fish

Here are some tips about purchasing frozen fish products:

§ Check that boxes are not squashed or torn. This can lead to freezer burn. Freezer burn is white or discolored patches on the flesh of a product that has been exposed to the air during freezing and storage. If applied to humans, we would call it frostbite.

§ When buying individually frozen fillets, check that there is not an overabundant glaze on the fish. This could mean that the product has been double dipped. This is the dishonorable practice of re-dipping frozen fillets in water to increase their weight. It is possible to buy in good faith a pound (500 g) of sole fillets, but on thawing be left with 12 ounces (375 g) of fish and 4 ounces (125 g) of very expensive fishy water.

§ When buying uncooked frozen shrimp, always buy them with the shell on because this keeps them fresh and naturally protected.

Buying Canned Fish

Even if they aren't at the top of your shopping list, tuna or salmon "butties" for the kids' lunches make a healthy alternative to peanut butter and jam. ("Buttie" is working class English for the Earl of Sandwich's famous creation — the sandwich.)

What other sorts of fish are canned? Well, there's mackerel (the basis of our famous mackerel pâté), sardines, pilchards and, not to be forgotten, anchovies (the heart of any good Caesar salad).

As thrifty housekeepers know, the art of good budgeting is "buying right." Therefore, when your local grocer has a special on canned salmon, stock up. When a hungry crowd of uninvited guests descends upon you, instead of reaching for the phone to order pizza, open a can of fish. Stir in a little mayo, spread on a slice of whole wheat bread, top with a lettuce leaf and — presto — you've got a wholesome, nutritious sandwich made in minutes.

Tuna is just as easy to prepare. Open the tin, drain off the liquid and place the contents in a bowl. Mash the tuna with a fork and then spread on toast. Top with grated cheese and place under the broiler for a tasty tuna melt.

One of our personal favorites is sardines in olive oil. Remove all the bones, mash into a paste and spread generously on hot buttered toast. It's a wonderful snack, breakfast or party nibble.

See how easy it is! By remembering to shop smart and by keeping canned fish handy, you'll always have something that's healthy and tasty for the family and, more importantly, something that will make up fast for unexpected company.

Cuts of Fish

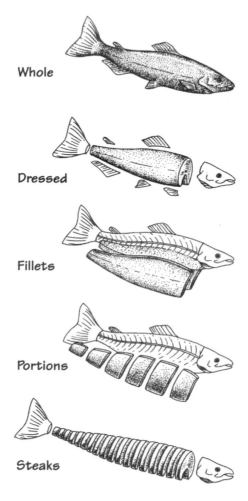

Whole

Dressed

Fillets

Portions

Steaks

Butterfly
Steak

Cuts of Fish

Whole (Drawn): Just as they come from the water with the insides removed. Scales may be taken off. Head and tail still on.

Dressed: As above, with head, tail and all fins removed.

Fillets: Fish cut lengthways from the backbone. Skin may be removed, but when left on, the fish breaks up less.

Portions: As above, with the fillet cut into approximately 8-oz (250-g) portions. Some fish, such as monkfish, tend to shrink when cooking, so we recommend buying a 10-oz (300-g) portion. With experience, you'll begin to recognize the perfect size fillet.

Steaks: A dressed fish, cut into 8-oz (250-g) cross sections ("darnes" is a fancy name for them).

Butterfly Steak: For a thinner steak, slice the steak in half from one side, leaving a hinge. Open and press flat. This cut is available from your fish supplier.

Preparing and Descaling Your Fish

So, armed with your newfound knowledge of fish, you now find yourself at the fishmonger. Shock, horror, gasp! So many fish, what shall we buy? Well, let's buy one of those beautiful Florida red snappers and a whole flounder from the North Atlantic. Before you buy, check them carefully. Check that the eyes are bright and full, not dull and sunken. Do they look like they have all their scales, with no bald

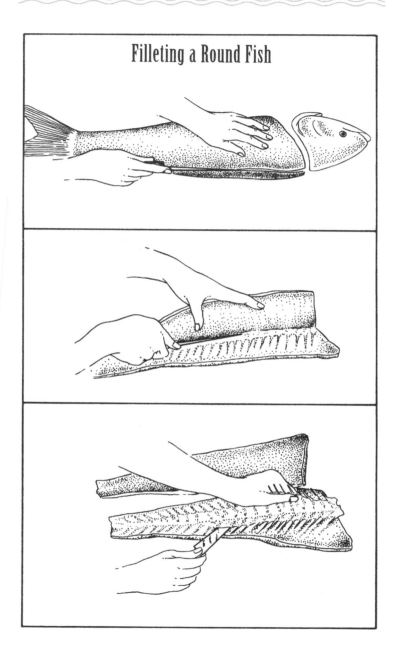

Filleting a Round Fish

patches? Bend down and smell them; they shouldn't smell unpleasant. Do they just smell like fish? If they pass your inspection, buy them.

At home, the fun stuff begins. Now you're going to clean and scale your first fish — the red snapper. Prepare your working surface by putting a chopping block on newspaper next to the sink. Get the salt, a good pair of kitchen scissors, a strong, medium-length cooking knife, and a fish scaler or, second best, a spoon. Run cold water into the sink and prepare a salt solution of 1 tbsp (15 mL) salt to 1 quart (1 L) cold water. Thoroughly submerge your fish in the cold water and wash the belly cavity carefully, removing any blood or tissue left behind. Next, place fishy on the chopping block.

Some people will tell you to descale the fish next, but we believe you should remove the fins first. The reason for this is simple. Just run your fingers along the fins of your red snapper. They're darn sharp, aren't they? Armed with your kitchen scissors, take hold of fishy by the tail (to get a better grip, dip your fingers in some salt), hold firmly and trim off the fins. Place the scissors as close to the body as possible, but be careful, don't cut the flesh of the fish. As with all things, practice makes perfect. Just take your time and you'll be a professional in no time.

Now that fishy is finless, we are going to remove its gills. Lay the fish on the chopping block and lift the gill cover or flap. Take your kitchen scissors and snip the gills. With your fingers, pull the gills away from the fish, turn over and repeat on the other side.

We talked about fun stuff earlier, well this is the really fun part — scaling the fish. Again, hold the fish by the tail and, working with the scaler or spoon, remove the scales from the tail toward the head in short, sharp strokes. Make sure you remove all the scales, especially around the anal and dorsal fin areas and the head and throat. Turn fishy over and descale the other side. When finished, rinse the fish under cold running water and gently shake until dry. Place the fish on a clean plate. It's now ready for cooking. Oh, by the way, if you followed all of our preparation hints, you'll know why we suggested you place newspaper on the work surface.

Don't worry, the fun doesn't stop here; you still have another fish to clean. Preparation for the flounder is much the same as for the red snapper; however, this fish is flat. You may want to remove the old scraps from your first fish and prepare a clean surface for this next job. Using your kitchen scissors again, trim the fins from tail to head and trim off the fins on both sides of the head. Next, lift up the gill cover and remove the gills. Wash the fish thoroughly in cold water. If you are going to cook the fish whole, it is now ready for cooking.

If you want to fillet the fish, this is what you do. Using your knife, make a V-shaped cut under the head through to the backbone on one side of the fish. Make the other side of the V-cut below the stomach cavity. Holding the top edge of the fillet in your free hand, press the knife flat against the rib bones and use a gentle sawing motion to remove the fillet. Turn the fish over, make another V-shaped cut and remove the fillet on the other side.

To skin a fillet, place the fillet skin side down on the working surface. Hold the fillet at the "tail" end and cut the skin away, holding the knife at a 45-degree angle, using short, sawing motions.

Filleting a Flat Fish

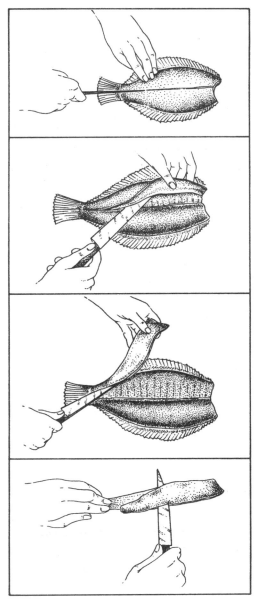

Helpful Hints about Purchasing Shellfish

Shellfish are divided into two groups of hard-shelled animals — mollusks and crustaceans. When purchasing either one, a good rule of thumb is that "fresh" means "live." It is obvious if a lobster is alive or not, but in the case of oysters, mussels and clams, the most important thing to look for is a firmly closed shell. This guarantees that they are not only fresh, but also still alive. If you follow these few simple rules, you won't go far wrong when purchasing fresh shellfish.

Buying Mollusks

Mollusks are small, hard-shelled fishy things that are not known for their ability to sprint. The only movement they make is the opening and closing of their shells. In this group are found oysters, mussels, clams and scallops.

Oysters: The food of lovers, kings and queens, rich and poor. Because there are many different varieties of oysters, we've chosen to highlight three of the most popular kinds that our customers have raved about.

NAME	SOURCE	SEASON
Malpeque	Prince Edward Island	July to December
Blue Point	Long Island, N.Y	All year, but best from September to April
Gulf Oyster	Gulf of Mexico, Florida to Texas	All year

To ensure that the oysters you buy are fresh, select only those with their shells tightly shut. In the world of fish, the expression for opening oysters is "shucking." Some tasty accompaniments to the oyster are seafood cocktail sauce, Tabasco sauce, horseradish sauce and lemon. However, some people like to top their oysters with a shot of vodka just to help them slip down more easily. This, in fish language, is called "an enjoyable experience."

Mussels: Mussels can be purchased wild or cultured. This doesn't mean they're party animals or have wonderful etiquette; it refers to their growing naturally or being farm raised. As wild mussels can be gritty or sandy, we recommend you purchase tightly closed cultured mussels; for example, P.E.I. mussels.

Clams: Two popular varieties are cherrystones and littlenecks. Cherrystones are much larger than other clams and are usually eaten raw on the half shell. Littlenecks are smaller and may be steamed in water, white wine, garlic, butter and finely chopped mixed veggies.

Scallops: Although mollusks, scallops are normally purchased "shucked" and in a ready-to-use state. Available year round, the best scallops come from Prince Edward Island and New Brunswick.

Scallops are purchased either as bay scallops, which are small, sweet and relatively inexpensive, or as sea scallops, which are larger, more delicate and graded by size. The size refers to the number of scallops per pound. They can be found graded as 10, 10-20, 20-30 or 30-40. All sizes of sea scallops are more expensive than bay scallops.

Buying Crustaceans

Crustaceans are shellfish that normally move about protecting themselves either with speed or pincers. In this group are lobster, crab and shrimp.

Lobster: Lobsters can be purchased all year round. They are fished from the Maritimes to Maine and are at their peak and cheapest to buy from late April to early June. Always purchase lobsters in a live state and avoid those that have soft shells. Soft shells are a result of the lobster preparing to shed its old shell so it can grow and replace it with a new, harder shell. Its flesh at this time is not at its best.

Crab: There are many varieties of crab available at different times throughout the year. The two most popular types, by far, are king crab and queen crab, available all year round in a frozen or precooked state.

King crab is sold by a size-to-price ratio. The number refers to the number of legs it takes to make up 10 lb (4.5 kg). The sizes are 14-16, 16-20 and 20-24. The price for size 14-16 is higher than for the other sizes because the legs are larger and meatier. Hence, bigger is best and bigger always costs more.

Queen crab, like king crab, is sold in three sizes: under 5, 5-8 and 8-12. The size refers to the weight of the leg clusters in ounces. The larger the number, the larger the cluster, and, again, the higher the price.

Both of these crabs are prepared for the table by boiling, broiling or steaming.

Shrimp: Do you know someone who doesn't like fish? But

they like shrimp — no, they love shrimp? It's hardly surprising because shrimp is the most popular seafood in the world today. There are many different varieties. Here are just a few:

American White Shrimp (Gulf Shrimp): These firm, white shrimp are probably the only shrimp available in a fresh state. They are being farmed more and more in order to broaden their availability.

Black Tiger: Fished and farmed all over the world, these firm shrimp are identified by a stripe or band around their grayish bodies.

Green Tiger: Like the black tiger shrimp, these shrimp are fished all over the world. However, this is a freshwater shrimp and, although it has an excellent taste, it is inclined to shrink alarmingly during cooking.

Pink Shrimp: Fished and farmed in the southern U.S., Caribbean and northern South America, these firm, pink shrimp are usually less expensive than other types of shrimp.

The sizing of shrimp is almost as complex as the varieties and sources of shrimp, so we'll keep it simple.

Salad Shrimp: If you want small shrimp for a salad, always buy coldwater shrimp (the best come from Quebec or the Maritimes). They come in three sizes — 125-175, 175-225 and 225-300. The smaller the number, the larger the shrimp. These shrimp are already cooked and shelled and should be allowed to defrost naturally overnight in the fridge or in a cool place. Never attempt to defrost them in hot water because this destroys their delicate taste.

Small to Medium-Sized Shrimp: The sizes of these shrimp refer to the average number of shrimp to the pound. Sizes 51-60, 41-50, 31-40 and 26-30 are used for sautéeing, deep-frying, broiling, steaming and peel 'n eat. Use your imagination; you'll love them.

Large Shrimp: These large-size shrimp are sized 21-25, 16-20, 13-15, 8-12 and under 4. As before, the sizes refer to the average number of shrimp to the pound. These shrimp are used in all the ways small and medium shrimp are used but, most importantly, are used for shrimp cocktails.

Well, if you can remember all that, you will have a good basic knowledge of fish. But don't worry; if you need help, just phone any Old Fish Market Restaurant manager and he will be pleased to assist you. You could even phone Balderick or myself if you can track us down. We like to keep on the move, however, following our principle that you can't hit a moving target!

Now you can try our recipes. Most of them are served in our restaurants, but some are new and will be introduced at later dates. Don't be afraid to experiment and, remember, if all else fails (and even if it doesn't), come visit us at the Old Fish Market. Baldrick will be only too pleased to cook you one of his specials and I will be only too pleased to supervise him to ensure: (1) that you get your entrée on the same day; (2) that he is not going to rattle his flag-day box in front of you; and (3) that he takes cash and not a case of beer as barter.

Popular Fish Choices

Type of Fish	Distinguishing Features	Place of Origin
Arctic Char	Olive-green to deep blue back, lighter green sides, orange-colored fins	N. Europe, NWT, Newfoundland, New Brunswick, Quebec
Atlantic Sole (Lemon Sole)	Flat fish, bought in fillets	Atlantic
Bluefish	White belly, silvery sides, greenish blue back	Florida, Caribbean, Gulf Stream
Butterfish	Gray-blue back and sides, silvery below	Atlantic, cool waters off Nova Scotia
Catfish	Whiskers on head, grayish blue skin	Fresh water, farmed
Cod	Grayish red with dark dots	Cold water, northern hemisphere
Croaker	Silvery below, greenish above, brownish spots on side	Atlantic
Cusk	Grayish skin	Cold water, northern hemisphere

TEXTURE OF FISH	TASTE	METHOD OF COOKING	CUTS
Firm meat, orangish color	Slightly oily	Broiled, panfried, barbecued, baked	Steaks, fillets
Soft meat	Mild	Panfried, baked	Fillets
Firm meat, darkish color	Slightly fishy	Broiled, baked	Fillets
Firm meat, rather bony	Mild	Broiled, barbecued, baked	Whole
Semi-soft meat	Delicate	Broiled, panfried, baked	Whole, fillets
White, flaky meat	Distinctive taste	Broiled, panfried, baked	Steaks, fillets
White, flaky meat	Mild	Broiled, barbecued, baked	Whole
White, flaky meat	Mild	Broiled, panfried	Fillets

TYPE OF FISH	DISTINGUISHING FEATURES	PLACE OF ORIGIN
Flounder	Flat fish, dark skin above, white below	Atlantic, cool waters
Grouper	Olive, bluish black, covered with dark blotches	Florida, Caribbean, saltwater
Haddock	Grayish green with a dark lateral line	Cold water, northern hemisphere
Hake	Grayish skin	Cold water, northern hemisphere
Halibut	Flat fish, black skin with small marks like bumps	Atlantic, cool waters
Herring	Silver skin, red eyes	Cool waters off Atlantic coast
Kingfish	Black skin	Gulf of Mexico, Florida coastline
Lake Trout	Silver skin, black spots	Throughout lakes in Canada
Mackerel	Black and silver markings	Atlantic, cool waters
Mahi Mahi	Blue, tough skin	Warm water, Hawaii

Texture of Fish	Taste	Method of Cooking	Cuts
White, semi-soft meat	Mild	Panfried, baked	Whole
Firm, soft meat	Delicate	Broiled, panfried, barbecued, baked	Fillets, butterfly cuts
White, flaky meat	Similar to cod	Broiled, panfried, baked	Fillets
Softer meat than cod	Slightly stronger tasting than cod	Broiled, panfried, baked	Fillets
White, semi-soft meat	Mild	Panfried, baked, barbecued	Steaks, fillets
Firm meat, bony	Strong	Panfried	Whole
Firm meat, oily	Strong	Broiled, baked, barbecued	Steaks
Orange, flaky meat, oily	Mild	Broiled, panfried, barbecued, baked	Fillets
Darkish, firm meat, oily	Very strong	Broiled, panfried, barbecued	Whole
Firm meat	Strong	Broiled, panfried, barbecued, baked	Steaks, fillets

Type of Fish	Distinguishing Features	Place of Origin
Marlin	Bluish black skin	Warm water, south coast U.S.A.
Monkfish	Pinkish meat	Caribbean
Mullet	White body with stripes	Pacific coast
Orange Roughy	White with reddish brown line down skin side of fillet	New Zealand, Australia
Perch, Lake	Yellow or green body, 6 to 8 vertical bars on sides	Found in many parts of North America
Pickerel	Olive brown or dark brown skin	Throughout Ontario, north toward Hudson Bay, northern Quebec
Pike, Northern	Green back, lighter green sides, white below	Great Lakes, throughout Ontario
Pollock	Greenish brown skin	Cold water, northern hemisphere

TEXTURE OF FISH	TASTE	METHOD OF COOKING	CUTS
Firm	Strong	Broiled, barbecued	Steaks
Firm	Similar to lobster	Broiled, panfried	Fillets, butterfly cuts
Firm	Strongish, distinctive	Broiled, baked, barbecued	Whole, fillets
Milky, firm meat	Mild, light	Broiled, panfried, baked	Fillets, mostly frozen
White, firmish meat	Highly esteemed, delicious flavor	Panfried, broiled, baked	Fillets
White, firmish meat	Distinctive	Panfried, broiled, baked	Fillets
White, flaky meat, rather bony	Mild	Broiled, panfried, barbecued, baked	Fillets
White, flaky meat	Similar to cod	Broiled, panfried, baked	Fillets

Type of Fish	Distinguishing Features	Place of Origin
Pompano	Bluish sides and back, silvery grading to yellow below	Caribbean, Gulf Stream
Porgy	Bright silver skin	Caribbean, Gulf Stream
Rainbow Trout	Green or greenish blue back blending to silvery on sides, white below, black spots on sides	Native to waters off Pacific coast, commercially farmed through-out Canada
Red Snapper	Bright red	Florida, Gulf of Mexico
Salmon	Different varieties: chum, coho, kokanee, chinook, etc.	Atlantic and Pacific
Sauger	Slender, brown or gray back, yellow sides overlaid with dark patches	St. Lawrence R. basin, throughout Great Lakes
Sea Bass, Black	Black coloring	Cool waters, Atlantic
Shad	Back is bright blue-green	Maritimes, Quebec
Shark	Black velvet-like skin	Atlantic, Pacific

TEXTURE OF FISH	TASTE	METHOD OF COOKING	CUTS
Firm meat	Strong	Panfried, baked, barbecued	Whole
Firm meat, rather bony	Strongish	Broiled, baked, barbecued	Whole
Whitish, firm meat	Excellent	Panfried, baked, barbecued	Whole
Firm meat, bony	Distinctive	Broiled, baked, barbecued	Whole
Pink and red, firm meat, oily	Distinctive	Boiled, poached, barbecued, baked	Whole, steaks, fillets
White, firm meat	Very flavorful	Panfried	Whole, fillets
Firm meat	Distinctive fishy flavor	Broiled, panfried, baked	Fillets
White, flaky meat	Highly esteemed	Broiled, panfried, baked	Whole
Firm meat, oily	Sweet	Broiled, baked barbecued	Steaks

TYPE OF FISH	DISTINGUISHING FEATURES	PLACE OF ORIGIN
Sheepshead	Dark green back, silvery sides, white belly	Great Lakes, except Superior
Skate	Normally sold skinned	Atlantic, cool waters, deep sea
Smelt	Slender, silvery	Rivers, lakes of Maritimes
Snapper. See Red Snapper; White Snapper		
Sole. See Atlantic Sole		
Splake or Wendigo	Cross between Lake Trout and Brook Trout, similar markings	Throughout lakes in Canada
Sturgeon, Lake	Dark gray to black with smooth skin	Upper St. Lawrence R., Lake Champlain, Great Lakes
Swordfish	Silver skin	Florida coast
Tilefish	Bluish, or greenish gray sprinkled with yellow spots, back and sides	Massachusetts to Virginia, Florida, Caribbean

TEXTURE OF FISH	TASTE	METHOD OF COOKING	CUTS
White, flaky meat	Good	Broiled, panfried, baked	Whole
Stringy meat, very perishable	Strong	Panfried	Wing cuts, center cuts
White, firm meat	Mild	Deep-fried	Whole
Orangish, flaky meat	Similar to lake trout	Panfried, broiled, barbecued	Fillets
Firm meat	Strongish, slightly oily	Broiled, panfried, barbecued, baked	Steaks
Brownish, firm meat, oily	Sweet	Broiled, barbecued	Steaks
Slightly flaky meat	Similar to grouper	Broiled, baked, barbecued	Fillets, butterfly cuts

TYPE OF FISH	DISTINGUISHING FEATURES	PLACE OF ORIGIN
Trout. See Lake Trout; Rainbow Trout		
Tuna	Dark red meat	Florida coast
Turbot	Flat, grayish green top, white underside	Atlantic
Whitefish	White skin with black markings	Widely in lakes
Whiting	Small, silvery, with dark lateral line	Atlantic
White Snapper	Silvery white	Florida, Gulf of Mexico
Winnipeg Goldeye	Yellow or gold eyes	Western Ontario

  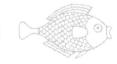 

Texture of Fish	Taste	Method of Cooking	Cuts
Red, firm meat; changes color when cooked	Strong	Broiled, baked, barbecued	Steaks, fillets
Firm	Mild	Panfried, boiled, baked	Fillets
White, flaky meat	Mild	Broiled or pan-fried, baked	Fillets
Firm meat, rather bony	Sweet	Panfried, barbecued	Whole
Flaky meat	Similar to red snapper	Broiled, baked, barbecued	Whole, fillets
Firm meat, bright orange skin when smoked	Very strong, slightly salty	Broiled	Whole

Conch Fritters

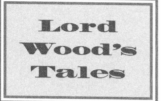
Lord Wood's Tales

When one thinks of conch, one thinks of warmer climates. Restaurants in the Bahamas and the Florida Keys serve this mollusk in salads or in a creamy chowder. Its flavor is similar to the clam's, but its meat is not as easy to get at. The meat is hidden in the conch's beautiful spiral-shaped shell, which is the size of two hands and is much sought after by shell collectors. Native people carved pictures on them and used them as trumpets; however, you don't have to do any of these things. Simply go to your local fishmonger and ask for conch meat. You pronounce it "konk."

1 lb	ground conch meat	500 g
1	egg	1
⅓ cup	milk	75 mL
1 cup	sifted all-purpose flour	250 mL
2 tsp	baking powder	10 mL
Pinch	salt	Pinch
½ tsp	celery seed	2 mL
5 to 6	drops Tabasco sauce	5 to 6
	Vegetable oil for frying	

1. Blend the ground conch, egg and milk together. This is best done in a food processor. In another bowl, sift the flour, baking powder and salt together and add to the conch mixture. Add the celery seed and Tabasco sauce. Mix thoroughly. It will have the consistency of a stiff batter.

2. Heat oil in a heavy skillet or electric frying pan. Allow about ⅓ cup (75 mL) of batter per fritter. Brown on both sides and drain well.

3. Serve hot with Tartare Sauce (page 142) or Spicy Cocktail Sauce (page 141).

Makes about 8 fritters.

Baldrick's Tips

When shallow frying, always fry the presentation side first.

Broiled Kiwi Clams

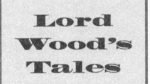

Lord Wood's Tales

This dish is a great appetizer and not only easy and readily available, but also expensive. Kiwi clams, as you might have guessed, come from New Zealand, home of orange roughy and the All Blacks. All very nice, although a little overrated. Kiwi clams are similar to our mussels, but they have a green shell (so would you if you traveled that far) and they tend to be a little larger.

You can use wild or cultivated mussels in place of the kiwi clams. Wild mussels are harvested from the natural ocean bed and rocks, whereas kiwi clams and cultivated mussels are grown in a controlled environment. Wild mussels have a little more flavor.

2 cups	grated Edam cheese	500 mL
4	slices bacon, sautéed and crumbled	4
24	kiwi clams, purchased open on the half shell	24
4	lemon wedges	4
	Fresh parsley sprigs	

1. Preheat broiler.

2. Mix the grated cheese with the bacon bits. Place the clams on a baking sheet and sprinkle with the cheese and bacon mixture.

3. Broil for 2 to 3 minutes until the cheese has melted and turned golden brown.

4. Place the clams in a circle on a small serving plate with the thin ends toward the middle. Place the lemon wedges on the side of the plate and the parsley in the middle.

Makes 4 servings.

Variation

Broiled Canadian Mussels

If you use good ol' Canadian mussels, as we would, wash them well and place them in a pot. Add water and 1 tbsp (15 mL) white vinegar, half covering the mussels. Add about 2 tbsp (25 mL) of chopped vegetables (whatever you have in the kitchen) and about ¼ cup (50 mL) of white wine (optional). Place over medium heat, cover and cook until the mussels are wide open. (This takes about 2 to 3 minutes.) Remove from pot and take off the top shell. Follow the recipe for Broiled Kiwi Clams.

Baldrick's Tips

Wild mussels need to be cleaned more thoroughly than cultivated ones. They sometimes have a little grit in them or even small crabs. After washing, cover the mussels with cold water. Stir in ¼ cup (50 mL) flour for every 2 cups (500 mL) cold water. Leave the mussels in the mixture for 4 to 6 hours, then wash them again in cold water.

Stuffed Mushroom Caps

Lord Wood's Tales

Stuffed Mushroom Caps are extremely easy to make and can be served as an appetizer at a dinner party or as an hors d'oeuvre at a cocktail party. They're also a great garnish for a salmon steak entrée. To add to your cooking pleasure, you could get up at the break of dawn and pick your own mushrooms, but be sure they're "fun guys" and not poisonous.

24	medium mushrooms	24
12 oz	snow crab meat	340 g
	Vegetable oil	
	Salt and pepper	
1 cup	Hollandaise Sauce (see page 140)	250 mL
4	lemon wedges	4
	Chopped fresh parsley	

1. Preheat broiler.

2. Wipe mushrooms, or wash and dry thoroughly. Remove stems.

3. Fill the caps with the crab meat and place on a greased baking sheet. Brush with oil and season with salt and pepper to taste.

4. Make Hollandaise Sauce and set aside.

5. Place the mushroom caps under the broiler for 2 to 3 minutes. Remove, drain and coat with the Hollandaise

Sauce. Place the caps briefly under the broiler to make sure they are nice and hot.

6. Arrange on a serving plate and garnish with lemon wedges and parsley.

Makes 4 servings.

Baldrick's Tips

If you don't have time to make Hollandaise Sauce, substitute grated cheese.

Mackerel Pâté

Lord Wood's Tales

This wonderful pâté has been served as a complementary appetizer at our restaurants for sixteen years. I don't know of any other restaurant serving it, maybe because it's become synonymous with the Old Fish Market.

1	can (15 oz/425 g) mackerel, well drained	1
2 tbsp	Mayonnaise (see page 141)	25 mL
1 tsp	sherry	5 mL
2 or 3	drops Tabasco sauce	2 or 3
	Salt and pepper	

1. In a mixing bowl, mash the mackerel with a fork. Add the rest of the ingredients and season to taste. Mix well.

2. Place in a small mold, chill until firm, and unmold onto a serving plate. Or spread on toast as a savory. Or use as a dip for nibbles.

Makes 6 servings.

Crab on Toast

Lord Wood's Tales

This is a very simple and appetizing dish, and there's not much more to say about it. Melba toast, a very thin crisp toast, was invented — no, not by Baldrick — but by that other "also ran" chef, Escoffier, who named it after the world-famous Australian diva Dame Nellie Melba. He also named a well-known peach dish after her.

1 cup	Cheese Sauce (see page 137)	250 mL
4	1-inch (2.5-cm) slices French bread	4
	or	
12	slices melba toast	12
8 oz	snow crab meat	250 g
4	tomato slices	4
	Salt and pepper	

1. Prepare the Cheese Sauce in the top of a double boiler and keep warm over hot water.

2. Preheat the broiler.

3. Toast the French bread on both sides. Spread the crab meat evenly over the toast. Place in a shallow ovenproof dish and cover with the Cheese Sauce. Place a slice of tomato on top of each piece and season with salt and pepper to taste. Grill until golden brown.

Makes 4 servings.

Variation:

Shrimp on Toast

Substitute shrimp for snow crab meat.

Baldrick's Tips

To peel a tomato, cut a small cross in the skin at the stem end, place in boiling water for 10 seconds, then in cold water. The skin will just peel away.

Anchovies on Toast

Lord Wood's Tales

This dish is usually served as a "savory" by the English. Considered a light dish, it can be served at the end of a meal in place of dessert. Baldrick and I are particularly partial to it, for as often as not when we are looking for something to eat, the kitchen is closed. Quick and easy, Anchovies on Toast satisfies those hunger pangs.

2	slices of bread, toasted	2
1	can (7 oz/198 g) anchovy fillets in olive oil, drained	1
4	pimiento-stuffed olives, sliced	4

1. Trim the crusts off the toast. Divide the anchovy fillets between the 2 pieces of toast and arrange lengthwise on each slice. Cut into triangles and garnish with olive slices.

Makes 2 servings.

Baldrick's Tips

Anchovies on Toast is a great nibble with lager or vintage port.

Baked Oysters

OYSTER TALK

"But wait a bit," The Oysters cried,
    "Before we have our chat;
For some of us are out of breath,
    And all of us are fat!"
"No hurry!" said the Carpenter.
    They thanked him much for that.

"A loaf of bread," the Walrus said,
    "Is what we chiefly need:
Pepper and vinegar besides
    Are very good indeed —
Now, if you're ready, Oysters dear,
    We can begin to feed."

From "The Walrus and the Carpenter" by Lewis Carroll

24	oysters on the half shell	24
12 oz	snow crab meat	340 g
1½ cups	grated Dutch cheese	375 mL
	(Edam or Gouda)	
4	slices bacon, sautéed and crumbled	4
1 cup	dry bread crumbs	250 mL
	Salt and pepper	

1. Preheat broiler.

2. Place oysters on a baking sheet. Place an equal amount of crab meat on top of each oyster.

3. In a bowl, combine the cheese, bacon bits, bread crumbs and salt and pepper to taste. Spoon the mixture onto the oysters.

4. Place the oysters under the broiler for 3 minutes or until browned. Remove from oven and serve.

Makes 4 servings.

Shucking an Oyster

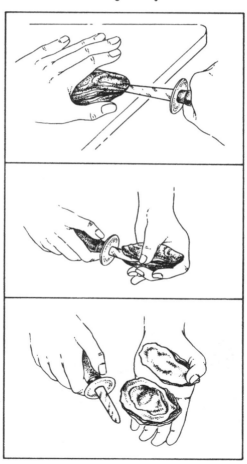

Angels on Horseback

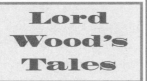

In our opinion, this is a much nicer appetizer or cocktail nibble than the similarly named Devils on Horseback, which consists of prunes wrapped in bacon.

24	oysters, shucked	24
12	slices bacon	12
4	slices bread, toasted lightly and buttered	4

1. Preheat broiler.

2. Wrap ½ strip of bacon around each oyster and secure with toothpick. Place on a baking sheet.

3. Place the oysters under the broiler until the bacon is crispy, turning once. Remove from oven and take out toothpicks.

4. Cut the crusts off the toast and divide each piece into 6 smaller pieces. Place each oyster on a piece of toast and serve.

Makes 4 servings.

Baldrick's Tips

The longer you cook oysters, the tougher they will be, so don't overcook them.

Shrimp Welsh Rarebit

Lord Wood's Tales

Welsh rarebit is basically cheese on toast. Ask most people in Wales what it is and they won't have any idea what you're talking about. I know this first hand as I have owned a restaurant in South Wales. Why a dish containing Irish beer and eaten by the English is called "Welsh" anything, I guess I will never know.

½ cup	dark beer (stout)	125 mL
1 cup	grated old cheddar cheese	250 mL
Dash	Worcestershire sauce	Dash
½ cup	whipping cream	125 mL
4	slices of bread, toasted	4
	Salad shrimp	

1. Preheat broiler.

2. Pour the beer into a small saucepan. Add the grated cheese and the Worcestershire sauce. Stir over medium heat until the cheese is melted. Add the cream and mix the ingredients together quickly and thoroughly. Remove from heat.

3. Thicken with beurre manié (see page 123).

4. Place the toast on a baking sheet. Spread the sauce over the toast and place under the broiler until nice and brown. Remove from oven, cut into triangles, and garnish with shrimp.

Makes 4 servings.

Cajun Popped Shrimp

Lord Wood's Tales

Cook plenty of these because they disappear at a rapid rate. Adding Cajun seasoning or lemon pepper to the batter only enhances this party favorite.

	Oil for deep-frying	
1	batch Basic Beer Batter	1
	(see page 75)	
1 lb	salad shrimp (175-225 size)	500 g
	Flour seasoned with salt and	
	pepper	
	Cajun seasoning	
4	lemon wedges	4
	Fresh parsley sprigs	

1. Pour the oil into the deep fryer and heat to 400° F (200° C). If you don't have a deep fryer, use a large, heavy saucepan and fill ⅓ full of oil.

2. Prepare the Basic Beer Batter and refrigerate for 1 hour before using.

3. Toss the salad shrimp in the seasoned flour. Shake off the excess flour and place the shrimp in the batter. Coat well. Take each shrimp out of the batter and toss into the fryer. Fry about 25 at one time until golden brown. Drain well and sprinkle with Cajun seasoning.

4. To serve, garnish with lemon wedges and parsley.

Makes 4 servings.

Garlic Shrimp

Lord
Wood's
Tales

This dish can be served as an appetizer or as an entrée. If served as an entrée, use the 26-30 size black tiger shrimp. Unfortunately, as the popularity of shrimp has grown, so too has the price. To our misfortune, our children's favorite appetizer is a shrimp cocktail.

16	black tiger shrimp (13-15 size), shelled and deveined	16
1 cup	butter, melted	250 mL
1 cup	mushrooms, sliced	250 mL
2	garlic cloves, chopped	2
Pinch	paprika	Pinch
4	lemon wedges	4
	Fresh parsley sprigs	

1. Wash shrimp under cold water and drain.

2. In a saucepan, melt the butter and add shrimp, sliced mushrooms and chopped garlic. Sauté for approximately 2 minutes, tossing frequently. Sprinkle a little paprika on top of the shrimp. Remove pan from heat.

3. Arrange the shrimp on a serving plate and pour the contents of the pan over them. To serve, garnish with lemon wedges and parsley.

Makes 4 servings.

Variation:

Garlic Scallops

Substitute large scallops for shrimp.

Deveining a Shrimp

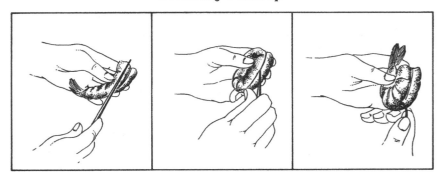

Baldrick's Tips

To devein shrimp, insert the tip of a sharp knife about ⅛ inch (.25 cm) into the shelledshrimp, slice down the length of the back and take out the vein.

Marinated Squid Rings

Lord Wood's Tales

Marinated Squid Rings are not only an excellent appetizer, but also a wonderful buffet dish or an accompaniment to barbecued meals in the summer.

Squid is one of the most intelligent and abundant marine organisms. Sometimes called calamari, which usually refers to the smaller squid, it is also one of the most versatile seafood items there is. Marinated, deep-fried or in fish stews, it is delicious. Mediterranean countries use squid in paellas and antipasto dishes. Its ink is used to flavor pasta and sauces. We would, however, not recommend filling your fountain pen with it.

1 lb	squid tubes, cleaned	500 g

Marinade

½ cup	red wine vinegar	125 mL
2 cups	vegetable and/or olive oil	500 mL
½ cup	red onion, chopped	125 mL
Pinch	dry mustard	Pinch
	Salt and pepper	
4	romaine leaves	4
4	tomato wedges	4
4	lemon wedges	4
	Chopped fresh parsley	

1. Cut squid into ¼-inch (.5-cm) rings. In a large saucepan, bring salted water to a boil. Add the squid and cook for 2 to 2½ minutes. Drain, rinse under running cold water, and drain again.

2. *Marinade:* In a bowl, combine the red wine vinegar and the oil. Add the red onion, dry mustard, and salt and pepper to taste. Mix well.

3. Add the cooked squid rings to the marinade and let stand for at least 12 hours in the refrigerator.

4. Place romaine leaves on a serving plate and pile the marinated squid on top. Garnish with tomato and lemon wedges and parsley.

Makes 4 servings.

Baldrick's Tips

You can play around with the marinade by using different vinegars and oils, but always keep the 4:1 ratio of oil to vinegar. Experiment with different mustards, too.

Neptune Breakfast Omelet

Lord Wood's Tales

The Neptune Breakfast Omelet is one of our most popular breakfast items, but we don't recommend making it for a large group because it can be time-consuming and you'll never get to eat one yourself. Instead, make one for a loved one and one for yourself.

3	eggs	3
	Salt and pepper	
1 tbsp	butter	15 mL
¼ cup	chopped onion	50 mL
3 oz	smoked salmon, diced	85 g

1. In a small bowl, whisk the eggs briefly and season with salt and pepper to taste.

2. In a small frying pan or omelet pan, heat the butter until bubbling. Sauté the onion in the butter until transparent. Pour in the eggs. Move the pan back and forth while stirring the eggs in a circular motion with a fork until cooked.

3. Sprinkle the smoked salmon on top. Fold both sides to the middle and turn out onto a warm plate.

Makes 1 serving.

Bouillabaisse

Restaurant critics love to impart their wisdom on this most noble of French dishes. They rate chefs on their ability to produce the perfect bouillabaisse. All the wisdom I can impart to you about bouillabaisse is this: use saffron, as many varieties of fish as you can, and fish stock or clam juice — never water.

¼ cup	olive oil	50 mL
¾ cup	chopped onion	175 mL
¾ cup	chopped celery	175 mL
1	garlic clove, chopped	1
1 lb	cod, turbot or halibut (the more varieties the better), skinless and boned	500 g
12	cultured mussels	12
½ lb	scallops (20-30 size)	250 g
½ lb	medium shrimp (26-30 size), shelled and deveined	250 g
12	littleneck clams	12
1	bottle (20 oz/591 mL) clam juice	1
	or	
2½ cups	Basic Fish Stock (page 60)	625 mL
1	can (19 oz/540 mL) peeled plum tomatoes, undrained, chopped	1
½ cup	dry red wine	125 mL
½ tsp	saffron powder	2 mL
	Salt and cayenne pepper	

1. Heat the oil in a large saucepan. Sauté the onion, celery and garlic in the oil until soft.

2. Cut the fish into pieces. Add the fish to the vegetables in the saucepan. Cook for 5 minutes, stirring occasionally.

3. Wash the mussels under cold water. Add the mussels, scallops, shrimp, clams, clam juice or fish stock, tomatoes with juice, and red wine to the saucepan and stir. Bring to a boil. Reduce the heat to simmer and season with the saffron and salt and cayenne pepper to taste. Simmer for 12 to 15 minutes. Discard any mussels that don't open before serving.

Makes 4 hearty servings.

Baldrick's Tips

The final touch to this meal is a bottle of dry, crisp French white wine and a loaf of French bread.

New England Clam Chowder

Lord Wood's Tales

Clam chowder originates from the Eastern seaboard, where it was a quick, cheap and nutritious way to feed hungry fishermen. There are many recipes for this soup and what you're served depends on where you are. In Manhattan, the clam chowder is tomato based. In New England, it has cream in it and in the Maritimes, cod. Over the years, the recipes have changed and what you might be served in one of the so-called designer restaurants may not contain any of the original ingredients, with the exception of the clams.

4	slices bacon, cut in small pieces	4
½ cup	chopped onion	125 mL
1 cup	diced potatoes	250 mL
2½ cups	Basic Fish Stock (page 60)	625 mL
1	can (8 oz/227 g) baby clams, drained but with juice set aside	1
Pinch	thyme	Pinch
Pinch	chopped fresh parsley	Pinch
½ cup	2% milk	125 mL
½ cup	whipping cream	125 mL
2 tbsp	butter	25 mL
	Salt and pepper	
	Paprika	

1. In a large saucepan, fry the bacon for a few minutes. Stir in the onion and cook until soft.

2. In another saucepan, cover the potatoes with water and bring to a boil. Simmer for 5 minutes. Drain the potato water into the pan with the bacon and onion, and set the potatoes aside.

3. Add the clam juice, thyme and parsley to the bacon mixture and bring to a boil. Reduce heat and simmer for 15 minutes. Stir in the milk and clams. Bring the mixture back to a boil and add the potatoes. Simmer for another 5 minutes. Remove from heat and slowly stir in the cream and butter. Season with salt and pepper to taste.

4. For a thicker chowder, use beurre manié (page 123).

5. Serve in a soup cup with paprika sprinkled on top.

Makes 4 hearty servings.

Baldrick's Tips

If you don't own a pepper mill, buy one. There's no substitute for freshly ground pepper.

Oyster Stew

Lord Wood's Tales

In ancient Greece, voters would cast their votes by marking their choice on the inside of an oyster shell. It wouldn't be a bad idea to bring this type of voting back into practice; it would surely cut down on government paper shuffling.

1 tbsp	butter	15 mL
24	oysters, shucked, set aside with juice	24
1 cup	chopped onion	250 mL
½ cup	white wine	125 mL
Dash	Worcestershire sauce	Dash
4 cups	2% milk	1 L
½ cup	whipping cream	125 mL
1 tbsp	chopped fresh parsley	15 mL

1. In a small saucepan, melt the butter. Stir in the oysters and their juice, the onion, white wine, and Worcestershire sauce. Bring to a boil.

2. In a medium saucepan, bring the milk to a boil and add the oyster mixture. Bring back to a boil. Remove from heat and slowly stir in the cream.

3. To serve, pour into soup dishes and garnish with parsley.

Makes 4 servings.

Shrimp in Beer

Lord Wood's Tales

What better way to enjoy shrimp than with the ever-so-popular beverage — beer. We do not, however, recommend drinking beer while cooking this recipe. One tends to spill too much. Baldrick, for example, has been known to eat up to a dozen of these dishes in one sitting, although we've noticed that he neglects to add the shrimp, butter, veggies, butter and parsley. He does use a soup dish, but only because he can't get his spoon into the bottle.

48	medium American white shrimp (51-60 size), shelled and deveined	48
¼ cup	butter	50 mL
½ cup	beer	125 mL
1 cup	mixed veggies (chopped celery, onion, carrot, red and green pepper)	250 mL
	Chopped fresh parsley	
½ cup	melted butter	125 mL

1. Combine all ingredients except melted butter and parsley in a saucepan. Cover and bring to a boil. Cook for 1 minute. Remove from heat.

2. To serve, pour into soup dishes, garnish with parsley and serve with melted butter for dipping.

Makes 2 servings.

Court Bouillon

Lord Wood's Tales

Court Bouillon is a regal-sounding name for an important part of many a dish. There are twenty different ways of making it. The one you use really depends on what you are preparing. Ours is suitable for most fish recipes. The most basic Court Bouillon is simply salt and water, which is used when cooking lobster. Come to think of it, maybe that particular way should have a name that's a little less regal.

2 tbsp	butter	25 mL
1	onion, coarsely chopped	1
1	carrot, coarsely chopped	1
1	celery stalk, coarsely chopped	1
8 cups	water	2 L
2	bay leaves	2
10 to 12	peppercorns	10 to 12
1 tsp	salt	5 mL

1. In a large saucepan, melt the butter. Sauté the veggies in the butter for 5 minutes. Add the remaining ingredients, bring to a boil, reduce the heat and simmer for 30 minutes.

2. Strain into a clean container and use as required.

Makes 8 cups (2 L).

Basic Fish Stock

A good Basic Fish Stock is an important ingredient in many fish recipes. Most restaurants and hotels use stock cubes rather than made-from-scratch stocks these days, but it's our belief that it's better to go the extra mile and make your own. Fish heads can be used, as well as bones, but some people are understandably a bit squeamish about them. Our advice? Just don't look in the pot while the stock is simmering!

2 tbsp	butter	25 mL
½ cup	chopped onions	125 mL
2 lb	sole, cod, halibut or turbot bones	1 kg
6	peppercorns	6
1	bay leaf	1
	Juice of ¼ lemon	
8 cups	water	2 L

1. In a large, heavy saucepan, melt the butter. Add the onions and cook for 1 minute until soft but not browned. Add the remaining ingredients except the water and cook for 5 minutes. Add the water and bring to a boil. Skim off any scum, reduce heat and simmer for 20 minutes; longer and the stock will become bitter.

2. Strain into a clean container and use as required.

Makes 8 cups (2 L).

Salads

Waldorf Shrimp Salad

Lord Wood's Tales

The Waldorf salad was developed in 1902 at the Waldorf-Astoria Hotel in New York City. To its standard ingredients, we've added shrimp.

4	Granny Smith apples, peeled, cored and cubed	4
	Juice of 1 lemon	
1 lb	salad shrimp	500 g
2 cups	diced celery	500 mL
½ cup	crushed walnuts	125 mL
1 cup	Mayonnaise (see page 141)	250 mL
1 cup	sour cream	250 mL
1	orange, peeled and segmented	1
	Romaine lettuce leaves	

1. In a bowl, mix the apples with the lemon juice. Drain. Add the remaining ingredients except the orange and romaine leaves. Mix together well.

2. To serve, lay romaine leaves on a serving plate and spoon the salad onto them. Garnish with orange segments.

Makes 4 servings.

Spinach Salad

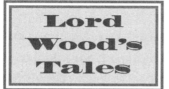

Lord Wood's Tales

Spinach might be hard to get your kids to eat, but just tell them what it did for Popeye. It might work for you. Our seven daughters weren't impressed!

Dressing

1½ cups	Mayonnaise (see page 141)	375 mL
¼ cup	lemon juice	50 mL
¼ cup	chopped red onion	50 mL
2	packages (10 oz/284 g) fresh spinach, washed, drained and stemmed	2
1 lb	salad shrimp	500 g
8	mushrooms, washed and sliced	8
¼ cup	walnut pieces	50 mL
4	slices bacon, sautéed and crumbled	4
4	lemon wedges	4
	Chopped green onions	

1. **Dressing:** In a bowl, combine the dressing ingredients and set aside.

2. Tear the spinach into bite-sized pieces and place in a salad bowl. Add the salad shrimp, mushrooms, walnuts and bacon bits, and toss with dressing.

3. To serve, garnish with lemon wedges and chopped green onions.

Makes 4 servings.

Baldrick's Tips

To make bacon bits, fry the bacon until crispy. Drain and chop as you would parsley. Refrigerate until ready to use.

Avocado and Shrimp Salad

Lord Wood's Tales

Avocados are tasty, healthy and, so our wives tell us, a great facial mask. Quite frankly, we're not sure why they would want to mash up a perfectly good avocado and put it on their faces. But since we both have beautiful wives, who are we to argue.

2	ripe avocados	2
	Romaine lettuce leaves	
8 oz	salad shrimp	250 g
½ cup	Marie Rose Sauce (page 140)	125 mL
4	sweet green pepper rings	4
4	lemon wedges	4
	Fresh parsley sprigs	

1. Cut the avocados in half. To keep them from wobbling on the plate, remove a small slice from the bottom. Place each avocado half on romaine leaves on a serving plate. Fill the cavity with the salad shrimp and coat with the Marie Rose Sauce.

2. To serve, garnish with the green pepper rings, lemon wedges and parsley.

Makes 4 servings.

Baldrick's Tips

To test an avocado for ripeness, be sure that there is a little give or softness at the end of the fruit. If it is soggy, the fruit is overripe.

Seafood Pasta Salad

Lord Wood's Tales

If I had to name one dish that has sprung into fashion recently it would be seafood with pasta — served cold or hot. This is a particularly delicious example of a cold pasta salad.

1	can (7 oz/198 g) tuna	1
4 cups	dried pasta (elbow macaroni or shells), cooked	1 L
1 cup	diced celery	250 mL
¼ cup	chopped onion	50 mL
2 tbsp	chopped fresh parsley	25 mL
	Salt and pepper	
¼ cup	sour cream	50 mL
¼ cup	prepared mustard	50 mL
2 tbsp	light cream	25 mL
2 tbsp	lemon juice	25 mL
2 tsp	honey	10 mL

1. Drain the fish and cut into bite-sized pieces. In a salad bowl, mix the fish with the pasta, celery, onion, parsley and salt and pepper to taste.

2. In a mixing bowl, combine the sour cream, mustard, cream, lemon juice and honey. Whisk until fluffy and light. Pour over the salad ingredients and mix thoroughly. Let stand for about 1 hour in the refrigerator before serving.

Makes 4 servings.

Baldrick's Tips

Shrimp, crab, salmon or smoked haddock can be substituted for the tuna in this recipe.

Catfish Fillets with Lemon Pepper

**Lord
Wood's
Tales**

Why the name "catfish" you might ask? Well, it doesn't have a soft, furry skin; in fact, it has just the opposite. Its skin is thick and slippery. It's not very comfortable on your lap and doesn't meow when you stroke it. But the catfish does have whiskers on either side of its mouth and I suppose it could look like a cat after a few glasses of wine.

More catfish are consumed in the United States than anywhere else in the world. Huge catfish pens are found in the southern states, particularly Louisiana. The most popular way to cook this fish is to deep-fry it or to marinate it in olive oil and Cajun seasoning, but we like this quick and simple lemon pepper recipe.

4	8-oz (250-g) catfish fillets	4
	Vegetable oil	
	Lemon pepper seasoning	

1. Preheat broiler.

2. Place the fillets on a greased baking sheet and brush with oil. Sprinkle generously with lemon pepper.

3. Broil for 3 minutes each side.

Makes 4 servings.

Baldrick's Clambake

Lord Wood's Tales

You've probably seen pictures of clambakes with scantily clad young men and women dancing around a beach fire with loud, head-banging music in the background. (Mmmm, maybe I'm not too old after all.) Anyway, clambake food is not cooked the way Baldrick says it is in his recipe. It is all steamed, preferably over wet seaweed. If you get the chance to have a clambake on the beach, do try it. It's such a healthy way to cook fish and seafood and you manage to keep all those delicate flavors sealed in the food. Another difference between Baldrick's clambake and mine is the cold beer. It's not really necessary, you know.

4	baking potatoes	4
40	littleneck clams	40
40	cultivated mussels	40
4	1-lb (500-g) lobsters	4
4	cobs of corn, husked	4
2 cups	butter, melted	500 mL
	French bread, heated	

1. Bake the potatoes until soft at 375° F (190° C) for 40 minutes to 1 hour, depending on their size.

2. Steam the clams, following the Steamed Mussels recipe on page 90. As the shells begin to open, add the mussels and cook for another 2 to 3 minutes until all the shells are open. Discard any mussels that don't open.

3. Follow the Cooked Lobster recipe on page 82 to cook the lobster.

4. In another pot, bring water to a boil and cook the corn.

5. Serve the clams and mussels with the melted butter and French bread.

6. Serve the lobster with the corn and baked potato and the rest of the melted butter.

7. Serve a salad with your favorite dressing and eat it at regular intervals or whenever you feel like it. Wash down regularly with cold beer and always leave room for a dessert or three!

Makes 4 servings.

Baldrick's Tips

If you do have a clambake on the beach, don't forget to let the clams stand in a bucketful of clear salt water for about 20 minutes before cooking. This will remove sand and mud.

Spicy Crab Cakes

Lord Wood's Tales

I came up with my own recipe for crab cakes. Even Baldrick is impressed with the results. I've kept the recipe fairly loose so that you can make your own interpretations.

2 tbsp	butter	25 mL
¼ cup	finely chopped onion	50 mL
1 lb	snow crab meat	500 g
1 cup	soft bread crumbs	250 mL
1 tsp	dry mustard	5 mL
1 tsp	Worcestershire sauce	5 mL
1	egg, beaten	1
Pinch	paprika	Pinch
	Juice of ½ lemon	
	Salt and pepper, to taste	
	Cajun seasoning or curry powder, to taste (optional)	
	Tabasco sauce, to taste (optional)	
	All-purpose flour seasoned with salt and pepper	
	Milk	
	Dry bread crumbs	
	Vegetable oil for frying	

1. In a frying pan, melt the butter and sauté the onion until soft.

2. In a bowl, combine the onion with the next 10 ingredients, mixing well. Divide the mixture into equal portions and roll into balls about the size of golf balls. Flatten with a spatula, dip in seasoned flour, then milk, then bread crumbs. Fry in a shallow layer of oil until nice and brown. Drain well and serve.

Makes about 20 crab cakes.

Dressing a Crab

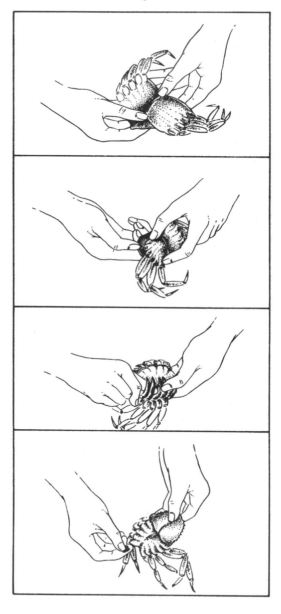

Soft-Shell Crab

Lord Wood's Tales

There are many different types of crab, from the king crab of Alaska to the soft-shell blue crab of the east coast. The one type that is especially interesting to me is the stone crab caught off the Florida coast. Fishermen are known to catch them, twist off a claw and then throw them back into the ocean. Cleverly enough, the stone crab proceeds to grow another claw. What a great business. My question is, why are stone crabs so expensive?

Soft-shell crabs are marketed in three sizes: hotel (small), prime (medium) and jumbo. All are prepared in the same way regardless of size. If you're going to serve them as an entrée, we suggest serving 3 or 4 medium crabs or 2 jumbo crabs per person. As an appetizer, serve 2 or 3 small crabs per person.

4	jumbo soft-shell crabs	4
1 cup	vegetable oil	250 mL
	All-purpose flour seasoned with salt and pepper	
	Lemon and lime wedges	
	Watercress	
	Clarified butter	

1. How to dress a crab (and not in a suit): Turn the crab on its back, lift the apron (the cover of the body) and remove it. Lift the flaps at each side and remove the gills. Cut off the eyes. Press above the legs and pull out the bile sac. Wash thoroughly in cold water and dry the crab on a paper towel.

2. Heat the oil in a frying pan until almost smoking. Dip the crabs in the seasoned flour and shake off any excess flour. Fry in the hot oil for approximately 5 minutes on each side and drain well.

3. Serve with lemon and lime wedges. Garnish with watercress. Clarified butter is a good accompaniment for dipping.

Makes 2 servings.

Baldrick's Tips

Soft-shell crabs must be fresh when you buy them because the shell hardens when taken out of salt water.

To clarify butter: Melt butter over low heat. Remove from heat and let stand, allowing the solids to settle to the bottom of the pan. The top layer is the clarified or "drawn" butter.

Fish Cakes

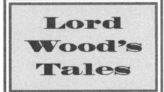

Lord Wood's Tales

On the California coast, fish restaurants compete on a daily basis to improve their crab cakes by using different species of crab, whole grain bread crumbs instead of white, and various seasonings. Baldrick, on the other hand, being of a simple nature, keeps his recipes simple, hence Fish Cakes.

1 lb	cooked fish (cod, halibut, turbot), skinned and boned	500 g
2	beaten eggs	2
2 cups	mashed potatoes	500 mL
	Salt and pepper	
	All-purpose flour seasoned with salt and pepper	
	Milk	
	Dry bread crumbs	
	Oil for frying	

1. In a bowl, mix the fish, egg and mashed potatoes together. Season with salt and pepper to taste. The mixture should be well bound together and stiff. If it isn't, add some soft bread crumbs. Divide the mixture into 10 equal portions and roll into balls. Flatten the balls with a spatula and dip in seasoned flour, then milk, then bread crumbs. Fry in a shallow layer of oil for 2½ minutes each side. Drain well and serve.

Makes 10 fish cakes.

Fish Pie

Lord Wood's Tales

Apple pie, meat pie, four and twenty blackbirds baked in a pie, but fish pie? Why not! It's a handy dish to make when you have one or two leftover fish fillets or steaks. You can always add canned fish if you don't have enough fillets.

1 lb	cooked fish	500 g
4	hard-cooked eggs, chopped	4
2 cups	Basic White Sauce (page 135), thinned with milk	500 mL
½ cup	chopped mushrooms	125 mL
	Smoked mussels or oysters (optional)	
	Salt and pepper	
2 cups	mashed potatoes	500 mL
	Milk	
	Chopped fresh chives	

1. Preheat oven to 350° F (180° C).

2. In a bowl, combine the first 5 ingredients. Season with salt and pepper to taste. Pour into a greased deep pie dish and spread the mashed potatoes on top. Brush with a little milk and bake for 20 minutes.

3. To serve, garnish with chopped chives.

Makes 4 servings.

Fish 'n Chips

We use halibut in our Fish 'n Chips, unlike so many other restaurants that use the cheapest fish they can find. We have found that its flavor and solid texture lend themselves wonderfully to deep-frying. Halibut is a little expensive but well worth it.

Basic Beer Batter

1 cup	all-purpose flour	250 mL
1 tsp	baking powder	5 mL
½ tsp	salt	2 mL
Pinch	pepper	Pinch
1	egg, beaten	1
1 cup	beer (preferably dark beer)	250 mL
	Oil for frying	
1½ lb	halibut (or cod, sole, haddock) fillets, cut into 8 thin slices	750 g
	All-purpose flour seasoned with salt and pepper	

1. ***Basic Beer Batter:*** In a bowl, mix the flour, baking powder, salt and pepper. Stir in the beaten egg. Gradually mix in the beer. If the mixture is lumpy, strain it. Place the batter in the refrigerator for 1 hour before using.

2. Preheat the oil in the deep fryer to 375° F (190° C). It must be this hot to set the batter and prevent it from becoming oil saturated.

3. Dip the fillets in seasoned flour and then in the Basic Beer Batter. Place rather than drop the fish in the hot oil. Dropping the fish might cause the oil to splatter, burning you. Fry until golden brown and crispy. (Don't fry too many pieces at one time.) Remove from the oil, drain well and serve with french fries.

Makes 4 servings.

Baldrick's Tips

When making french fries from fresh potatoes, cook the potatoes in clean oil at 325° F (160° C) for 3 to 4 minutes. Remove from the oil and refry at 375° F (190° C) until crisp and golden.

When cooking Fish 'n Chips, cook the fish in the same oil as the french fries.

Grouper with Pepper Sauce

Lord Wood's Tales

Did you know that the grouper changes sex, or so Baldrick tells me. He saw it on a T.V. show, so it must be true! Anyway, the grouper is a big, tasty fish, which folks in the southern United States like to turn into fish fingers. Part of the sea bass family, it can reach up to 6 feet (2 m) in length and weigh 500 pounds (225 kg). However, it usually weighs about 15 pounds (7 kg) when fully grown. Cut into steaks, it's great eating and one of our favorites. (P.S. He's right! The grouper changes from female to male. It's a funny old world down there.)

4	8-oz (250-g) grouper fillets or steaks, skinned	4
½ cup	crushed black peppercorns	125 mL
½ cup	butter	125 mL
½ cup	chopped onion	125 mL
½ cup	chopped sweet green pepper	125 mL
½ cup	chopped sweet red pepper	125 mL
½ cup	brandy	125 mL
1 cup	whipping cream	250 mL
1 tsp	Tabasco sauce	5 mL
1 tsp	Worcestershire sauce	5 mL

1. Wash the grouper fillets or steaks under cold water and pat dry with a paper towel. Rub the crushed peppercorns into the fish.

2. Melt the butter in a frying pan. When it is hot, add the fillets and cook 4 to 5 minutes on each side. (Allow a little longer if the fillets or steaks are thick.) Remove the fish from the pan and keep warm.

3. Add the onion, green pepper and red pepper to the pan and sauté for 2 to 3 minutes or until soft. Drain off the butter and return pan to the heat. Add the brandy and flambé. When the flames have died off, stir in the cream, Tabasco sauce (if you like it hot, add more!) and Worcestershire sauce. Bring to the boiling point, reduce heat immediately and return the grouper to the pan. Turn the fillets after 2 minutes. Cook for a further ½ minute, remove from the sauce and place on a serving plate. (For a thicker sauce, allow the sauce to simmer for a couple of minutes longer.) Coat the fish with the sauce and serve.

Makes 4 servings.

Baldrick's Tips

When serving food, always ensure that the plates are hot for hot food and cold for cold food.

Smoked Haddock Kedgeree

Lord Wood's Tales

This wonderful dish can be served for breakfast, lunch or dinner. It was at the height of its popularity in the Victorian era when the sun never set on the Empire. No breakfast buffet was complete without kedgeree. For some reason, it never really made it to North America.

2 cups	milk	500 mL
2 cups	water	500 mL
2 lb	smoked haddock	1 kg
4	hard-cooked eggs	4
2 cups	cooked white rice	500 mL
½ cup	butter	125 mL
	Salt and pepper	
2 cups	Curry Sauce (page 138)	500 mL

1. In a saucepan, bring the milk and water to a boil. Add the smoked haddock and return to boil. Reduce heat, cover the pan and poach for 5 to 6 minutes. Remove fish and let cool.

2. Chop the eggs into ¼-inch (.5-cm) pieces. Remove skin and bones from the fish and break it up into flakes. Mix the fish, egg and cooked rice together in a saucepan. In another saucepan, melt the butter and add to the fish mixture. Heat thoroughly for 5 minutes. Season with salt and pepper to taste.

3. Serve with Curry Sauce.

Makes 4 servings.

....

Variation:

Salmon Kedgeree
Substitute salmon for the smoked haddock.

Baldrick's Tips

John likes to mix the Curry Sauce with the kedgeree rather than serving it on the side.

Orange-Marinated Halibut Steak

Lord Wood's Tales

Now if you want to see a really big fish, look no further than the halibut. How big is it? About 10 feet (3 m) long and 400 pounds (180 kg). Halibut that weigh over 100 pounds (45 kg) are known as whale halibut. This flat fish swims deep in the ocean and is part of the same family as the sole.

Orange Marinade

2 cups	orange juice concentrate, defrosted	500 mL
½ cup	sherry	125 mL
½ cup	soya sauce	125 mL
2	cloves garlic, crushed	2
4 tsp	olive oil	20 mL
4	10-oz (300-g) halibut steaks	4
1 cup	soft bread crumbs	250 mL

1. *Orange Marinade:* In a large dish, combine the orange juice concentrate, sherry, soya sauce, garlic and olive oil.

2. Marinate the halibut in the Orange Marinade in the refrigerator for at least 2 hours.

3. Place the steaks on a greased baking sheet and sprinkle with the bread crumbs. Bake in the oven at 350° F (180° C) for approximately 20 minutes, basting twice with the marinade. The fish will be done when it flakes easily with a fork.

Makes 4 servings.

Baldrick's Tips

When creating a menu, balance is important. Never serve a fish appetizer with a fish entrée.

Cooked Lobster

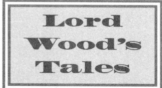

Lobster, that King of Crustaceans! Cooked alive and then eaten minutes later, lobster is a sweet, succulent and satisfying meal for lovers to share and gourmands to savor.

1	1 to 1½ lb (500 g to 750 g) live lobster	1
2 tbsp	salt	25 mL
	Clarified butter (see page 72)	

1. Place the lobster in a large saucepan filled with boiling, salted water. Cover and cook for 10 to 12 minutes. Lift the lobster from the water and drain well. Split the tail and crack the claws.

2. Serve with "lashings" of clarified butter.

Allow 1 lobster per person.

Baldrick's Tips

We would strongly suggest wearing a lobster bib when eating these beauties as they are apt to be a bit of a challenge. When cracking open the lobster, the juice can spray around quite liberally. (My Lord Wood needs to use a bath towel.) When you finally get around to eating, don't forget the meat in the legs.

Lobster Thermidor

The female lobster is better tasting than the male, although either sex is preferred over the crayfish or spiny lobster, which has no claws and is found off the coast of Florida. Our lobsters come from either Prince Edward Island or Maine.

4	1 to 1½ lb (500 g to 750 g) Cooked Lobsters (page 82)	4
½ cup	butter	125 mL
½ cup	finely chopped onion	125 mL
¼ cup	all-purpose flour	50 mL
1 cup	whipping cream or 2% milk	250 mL
2 tsp	dry mustard	10 mL
1 cup	grated Parmesan cheese	250 mL
½ cup	brandy	125 mL
	Salt and pepper	

1. After the lobsters are cooked, plunge them into cold water to stop the cooking. Following the diagram on page 84, split the lobster and clean the body cavity. Remove all of the lobster meat from the shells and claws. Chop the meat into bite-sized pieces. Wash the lobster shells and set aside.

2. In a saucepan, melt ¼ cup (50 mL) of the butter. Sauté the onion in the butter until transparent. Add the flour and mix thoroughly over low heat for 30 seconds. Slowly stir in the cream or milk, using a whisk, and bring to a boil. Stir in the dry mustard and ½ cup (125 mL) of the Parmesan cheese, mix well and remove from heat.

Preparing a Lobster

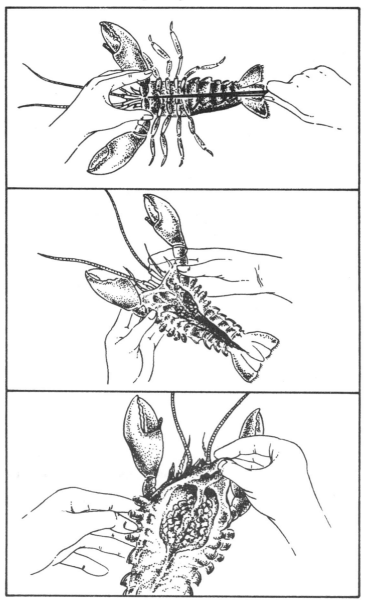

3. Preheat broiler.

4. In a sauté pan, melt the remaining butter and add the lobster meat. Stir quickly for a few seconds, add the brandy and flambé. When the flames have died down, add the sauce to the lobster meat and mix well. Season with salt and pepper to taste. Place the lobster shells on a baking sheet and fill the cavities with the mixture. Sprinkle with the remaining Parmesan cheese and brown under the broiler for 2 minutes until golden and bubbly.

Makes 4 servings.

Baldrick's Tips

Always keep knives sharp. The worst wounds are caused by dull knives. If you don't own a good knife sharpener, buy one.

Hawaiian Mahi Mahi
(Not Flipper, but His Cousin)

Lord Wood's Tales

When we first put this dish on our menu and sold it as "dolphin," we received complaint phone calls and not very nice letters. It's taken a long time and a name change to convince people that we never did nor ever will serve Flipper. Dolphin, the fish rather than the porpoise, is well known in Hawaii and Japan, where its delicate flavor and moist, solid texture make it very popular.

4	8-oz (250-g) mahi mahi fillets	4
	Vegetable oil	
	Salt and pepper	
4 tsp	cornstarch	20 mL
2 cups	pineapple juice	500 mL
4 tsp	shredded coconut	20 mL
8	rings of canned pineapple	8

1. Preheat the broiler.

2. Brush both sides of each fillet with oil and season with salt and pepper. Broil for 4 to 5 minutes per side.

3. In a small bowl, mix the cornstarch with ¼ cup (50 mL) of the pineapple juice. Set aside.

4. In a saucepan, combine the remaining pineapple juice and the coconut and bring to a boil. Stir in the cornstarch mixture and mix well until the sauce thickens.

5. To serve, place each fillet on a serving plate, coat with the sauce and garnish with pineapple rings.

Makes 4 servings.

Baldrick's Tips

Get to know your fishmonger, who will be able to introduce you to many exciting varieties of fish.

Marlin with Barbecue Sauce

Lord Wood's Tales

Imagine getting up each morning off the coast of Florida, going down to your boat and setting off to catch this beautiful 400-pound (180-kg) fish. You can "sport fish" it, eat it or even hang it on the wall as a decoration.

Barbecue Sauce

½ cup	dry red wine	125 mL
½ cup	tomato paste	125 mL
¼ cup	water	50 mL
2	large cloves garlic, crushed	2
2 tbsp	hot prepared mustard	25 mL
2 tsp	chili powder	10 mL
2 tsp	Worcestershire sauce	10 mL
4	8-oz (250-g) marlin steaks	4
	Chopped green onion	

1. ***Barbecue Sauce:*** Combine all the ingredients in a saucepan. Bring to a boil and simmer for 5 minutes, stirring frequently.

2. Preheat the broiler or barbecue.

3. Place the steaks on a greased baking sheet or on the barbecue grill. Baste the marlin with the sauce and grill for 3 to 4 minutes on each side, or until a fork can be inserted easily into the steaks. Baste regularly.

4. To serve, place on a serving plate and spoon on hot
sauce. Garnish with chopped green onion. Remaining
sauce may be served on the side or refrigerated for
later use.

Makes 4 servings.

Sweet 'n Sour Monkfish

Lord Wood's Tales

Another one of those fish with
numerous names is the monk-
fish. One look at this little devil and
you can understand why it has so
many names; it's incredibly ugly.
Would you eat goosefish, frogfish or monkey fish? Well,
they're all the same fish. Its taste, however, makes up for its
looks. It tastes somewhat like lobster. And, yes, poor man's
lobster is another name for monkfish.

2 lb	monkfish fillets, cut into ½-inch (1-cm) cubes	1 kg
1	batch Basic Beer Batter (page 75) Oil for deep-frying	1

Sweet 'n Sour Sauce

1	can (14 oz/398 mL) of pineapple cubes in its own juice, undrained	1
1½ tbsp	cornstarch	20 mL

¼ cup	ketchup	50 mL
¼ cup	vinegar	50 mL
½ tsp	soya sauce	2 mL
1	carrot, peeled and cut in julienne strips	1
1	stalk celery, cut in julienne strips	1
1	sweet green pepper, cut in julienne strips	1

1. Prepare the fillets and Basic Beer Batter. Deep-fry the monkfish following the method used in the Deep-Fried Shrimp recipe on page 116.

2. *Sweet 'n Sour Sauce:* Drain the pineapple, reserving the juice. Mix the juice and the cornstarch in a saucepan. Stir in the ketchup, vinegar and soya sauce. Bring to a boil slowly, stirring constantly. Add the vegetables and simmer for 5 minutes. (If you find the sauce is too tart, add a little sugar.)

3. Add the cooked, well-drained monkfish balls to the sauce and serve.

Makes 4 servings.

Baldrick's Tips

The only part of the monkfish that is normally for sale is the tail. It tends to shrink as it cooks, so if you want an 8-oz (250-g) portion, you should buy 10 oz (300 g) of the raw fish.

Steamed Mussels

Lord Wood's Tales

Steamed mussels can be served as an entrée or as an appetizer. French bread for dunking and a nice crisp dry white wine make this dish an experience not to be missed.

1 lb	cultured mussels	500 g
¾ cup	Basic Fish Stock (page 60) or water	175 mL
¼ cup	white wine	50 mL
½ cup	chopped veggies (celery, onion, carrot, sweet red and green pepper)	125 mL
1	clove garlic, minced (optional)	1
	Chopped fresh parsley	
¼ cup	melted butter	50 mL

1. Scrub the mussels well under cold water.

2. In a large, heavy pot, combine the Basic Fish Stock or water, wine, veggies and garlic (if using). Cover and bring to a boil. Boil for 2 minutes. Add the mussels and simmer, covered, for 4 to 5 minutes, or until the mussel shells open completely. (Discard any that don't open.) Pour mussels and liquid into a soup tureen and top with chopped parsley.

3. Serve with melted butter on the side for dipping.

Makes 1 serving.

Baldrick's Tips

The two main species of mussels are the common blue and green mussels; the latter has a larger shell. When choosing mussels, beware the wild blue mussel, which is not as good as the well-bred cultured one.

Orange Roughy with Kiwifruit

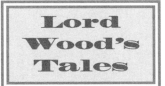
Lord Wood's Tales

Would you buy a fish called slime head? I bet you have and even eaten it, too. Some bright spark of a marketing person decided to call it orange roughy, probably because it looks orange when it's caught. It has become the non-fish-lover's fish. It's white, light, boneless and delicate in flavor. Orange roughy comes from New Zealand and we were one of the first restaurants to put it on our menu.

4	8-oz (250-g) orange roughy fillets	4
	Vegetable oil	
	Salt and pepper	
4	kiwifruits, peeled and sliced	4
2	oranges, peeled and sectioned	2
	Chopped fresh parsley	

1. Preheat broiler.

2. Place the fillets on a greased baking sheet. Brush with vegetable oil and season with salt and pepper to taste. Grill for 5 to 6 minutes, or until flesh flakes easily when pierced with a fork.

3. To serve, garnish with kiwi and orange slices and chopped parsley.

Makes 4 servings.

Baldrick's Tips

O range roughy is available for the most part in frozen fillets. Don't keep store-bought frozen fish longer than a month before using.

Steak and Oyster Pie

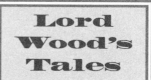

Lord Wood's Tales

This dish puts a new slant on that old favorite, the meat pie. The blend of oyster juice and the juices from the sirloin will captivate even the dullest of taste buds.

¼ cup	vegetable oil	50 mL
1½ lb	lean sirloin beefsteak, cut into ½-inch (1-cm) cubes	750 g
½ cup	chopped onion	125 mL

¼ cup	all-purpose flour	50 mL
2 cups	beef stock	500 mL
¼ cup	tomato paste	50 mL
12	oysters, shucked	12
	Pastry for single-crust 10-inch	
	(25-cm) pie	
	Milk	

1. Heat oil in a saucepan. Add steak cubes and onion. Stir until meat is browned. Add the flour and stir well over low heat for 2 minutes. Stir in the beef stock and tomato paste. Bring mixture slowly to a boil, stirring frequently. Reduce heat to low and cook for 1½ to 2 hours, stirring occasionally. Remove from heat and let cool.

2. Pour cooled meat mixture into a pie plate and arrange oysters on top. Cover with the pie pastry, prick with a fork in several places to allow steam to escape, and brush with milk. Bake in a 375° F (190° C) oven for 30 minutes.

Makes 4 servings.

Baldrick's Tips

To make the lightest pastry, pass the flour through a sieve first.

Poached Whole Salmon

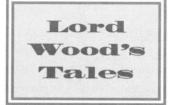

Lord Wood's Tales

Baldrick and I were on the "Bob McLean Show" in the Windsor area once and Bob asked Baldrick what the difference was between Atlantic and Pacific salmon. Baldrick, not missing a beat, retorted, "Oh, about 3,000 miles." "No really, Chef," said Bob, "what's the difference?" Baldrick replied, "Really, Bob, about $2 a pound." Now perhaps you can understand what all of us at the Old Fish Market have to put up with. At least he can cook!

1	5 to 6 lb (2.5 to 3 kg) salmon	1
8 qt	Court Bouillon (page 59)	8 L
2	pimiento-stuffed olives	2
1	English cucumber	1
6	lemons	6
1	head lettuce, finely chopped	1
6	hard-cooked eggs, quartered	6
	Fresh parsley sprigs	
	Mayonnaise (see page 141)	

1. Clean the salmon as described on page 13, leaving the head on.

2. Prepare the Court Bouillon in a large fish kettle, roasting pan or saucepan. Place the salmon in it. If the bouillon doesn't cover "fishy," top up with water and vinegar using a ratio of 1 part vinegar to 10 parts water. Bring slowly to a boil and simmer gently for 12 minutes.

Remove from heat and allow the salmon to cool in the liquid. After it has cooled, carefully place it on a large serving tray. Using a small knife, scrape off the skin, remove the eyes, fins and gray, fatty portions and discard. Refrigerate until ready to decorate.

3. To decorate your salmon, place the olives in the eye sockets. Slice the cucumbers and 3 of the lemons. Starting at the head, alternate cucumber and lemon slices down the length of the fish. Surround the salmon with the shredded lettuce and garnish with the remaining lemons cut into wedges, hard-cooked eggs and parsley. Serve with Mayonnaise.

Makes 10 to 12 servings.

Baldrick's Tips

"Why on earth would you want to cook a whole salmon?" you may ask. Well, in my opinion, if you're giving a party, why would you want to spend all your time in the kitchen when you could lay out a buffet, using a beautiful salmon as your centerpiece? That way, you get to eat and make merry. After all, since you're the one who's paying, why not enjoy your own party?

Smoked Salmon Fettuccine

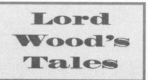

Lord Wood's Tales

We are the proud inventors of Smoked Salmon Fettuccine and, for the past five years, it has been one of our most popular items in Coasters, our shellfish bar.

½ cup	butter	125 mL
4	cloves garlic, chopped	4
1 lb	smoked salmon, diced	500 g
1 cup	whipping cream	250 mL
4 cups	fettuccine noodles, cooked and kept warm	1 L
½ cup	Parmesan cheese	125 mL

1. In a saucepan, melt the butter. Add the chopped garlic and smoked salmon. Cook over high heat, stirring constantly, for 2 minutes. Add the cream to the salmon mixture, stir until heated and pour over hot noodles. Sprinkle the Parmesan cheese on top and serve.

Makes 4 servings.

Baldrick's Tips

This is such a simple dish to make that even My Lord Wood can do it, or so he tells me. Smoked salmon bits can be bought at your local market or, if you can't find them, dice slices of smoked salmon.

Poached Salmon Steaks

Lord Wood's Tales

When Baldrick and I sat down and I said, "Baldrick, it's time to talk about poaching," before I could put the poor chap right, he spent five minutes telling me to get out of bed at midnight, remember where I'd set my traps the previous night, and always, always have an alibi. I didn't think our readers would be interested in his nocturnal habits, so I said, "Cooking, Baldrick, cooking."

	Court Bouillon (page 59)	
4	8-oz (250-g) salmon steaks	4
8	cucumber slices	8
4	lemon wedges	4
	Fresh dill	

1. In a large saucepan, make enough Court Bouillon to cover the salmon steaks. Bring it to a boil. Add the salmon steaks and return to the boil. Immediately reduce the heat so that the liquid is just simmering, not boiling. Cook for approximately 5 minutes (if the steaks are thick, poach a little longer). Lift the salmon steaks carefully from the liquid and drain well.

2. To serve, garnish with cucumber slices, lemon wedges and dill.

Makes 4 servings.

Baked Salmon Steaks

This is a fantastic way to cook salmon. All the flavors blend together and are trapped in the foil "bags." We have a lot of friends (that in itself is fantastic!) who cook salmon on the barbecue this way. Try this dish alfresco in the summer – it's a welcome change from hamburgers and hotdogs.

4	8-oz (250-g) salmon steaks	4
½ cup	olive oil	125 mL
¼ cup	lemon juice	50 mL
1 tsp	dried marjoram or dried thyme	5 mL
	Salt and pepper	
4	slices lemon or lime	4

1. Preheat oven to 450° F (230° C).

2. Measure out 4 pieces of aluminum foil approximately 4 times the size of the salmon steaks. Brush each piece of foil with a little olive oil and place a salmon steak in the middle. Fold the ends of the foil up toward the steak and then fold the sides toward the middle, leaving the top open.

3. In a bowl, combine the remaining olive oil, lemon juice, marjoram or thyme, and salt and pepper to taste. Pour over each salmon steak, place a lemon slice on top and close the top of each "bag" by pinching the foil together.

Place the "bags" on a baking sheet and bake for 20 minutes, or until salmon is opaque throughout.

Makes 4 servings.

Variations:

The recipe can be varied by using different herbs, such as fresh dill.

$\mathscr{G}$ravlax

This dish originates in Scandinavia where the refrigeration part was done below ground. The salmon, wrapped in cloth, was placed in a hole, covered with soil and left for two days.

3 lb	fresh salmon fillet	1.5 kg
¼ cup	salt	50 mL
½ cup	sugar	125 mL
1	bunch fresh dill, coarsely chopped	1
2 tsp	white peppercorns, crushed	10 mL
	Butter	
	Cucumbers, sliced	
	Fresh dill sprigs	
	Lemon wedges	

1. Cut the fillet into 2 equal pieces. Do not rinse; pat dry with paper towels.

2. In a bowl, combine the salt and sugar. Rub the fish with some of this mixture.

3. Sprinkle some of the salt and sugar mixture and some of the chopped dill on a large piece of aluminum foil. Place one piece of salmon, skin side down, on the mixture and sprinkle generously with dill, crushed peppercorns and the salt and sugar mixture. Cover with the second piece of salmon, skin side up. (If the pieces do not match in shape, place the thick side of one piece against the thin side of the other piece.) Sprinkle with the remaining salt and sugar mixture. Wrap the fish in the foil and place it in a baking dish. Put a light weight on top. Refrigerate.

4. After about 4 to 5 hours, pour off the fluid. Keep the Gravlax refrigerated for at least 48 hours, turning the fish over at least twice during that period. It can be stored for a week in the refrigerator.

5. To serve, slice the salmon thinly, removing the skin. Sauté the skin in butter, roll it up and use as a garnish in addition to sliced cucumbers, dill sprigs and lemon wedges.

Makes 12 servings.

Simple Salmon or Tuna Soufflé

Lord Wood's Tales

Making a soufflé is the supreme test of skill for any chef. Can you make it rise and can you keep it like that until it's time to serve it? This tried-and-true recipe will succeed as long as you follow the directions carefully. The secret? Beat the egg whites well to get lots of air into them. To test that the egg whites are stiff, just turn the bowl upside down. If they fall out onto the floor, you know they're not stiff enough!

2 tbsp	butter	25 mL
1	green onion, chopped	1
1	can (10 oz/284 g) condensed cream of mushroom soup	1
6	large eggs, separated	6
2	cans (7 oz/198 g) salmon or tuna, drained	2

1. Preheat oven to 350° F (180° C).

2. In a large saucepan, melt the butter and sauté the green onion for 2 minutes or until soft. Stir in the can of mushroom soup and cook over low heat for 2 to 3 minutes, mixing thoroughly. Remove from heat.

3. In a bowl, beat the egg yolks for about 2 minutes. Slowly stir them into the soup mixture and place over low heat. Stir constantly until mixture thickens and resembles custard. Remove from heat.

4. Mash the salmon or tuna and add it to the soup mixture.

5. Grease a medium soufflé dish with butter and dust with flour. Beat the egg whites in a clean, grease-free bowl until very stiff. Fold the egg whites into the soup mixture with a spatula. Fill the soufflé dish three-quarters full with the mixture and place the dish in a roasting pan. Fill the pan half full with boiling water. Bake for 15 minutes at 350° F (180° C), increase the temperature to 400° F (200° C) and bake for another 30 to 40 minutes, until the top is golden brown and the center is solid. Serve immediately.

Makes 4 servings.

Baldrick's Tips

Never beat egg whites in an aluminum or plastic bowl.

Salmon or Tuna Lasagne

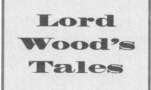

Lord Wood's Tales

Yes, fish gets into everything, even lasagne. But as we tell our patrons, "Don't knock it until you've tried it." It's one of those fish dishes you don't have to spend time watching, turning or worrying about when it's cooking.

1 tbsp	olive oil	15 mL
½ cup	finely chopped onion	125 mL
2	cloves garlic, minced	2
1	can (14 oz/398 mL) tomatoes, undrained	1
1	can (7½ oz/213 mL) tomato sauce or spaghetti sauce	1
½ tsp	dried rosemary	2 mL
½ tsp	dried oregano	2 mL
½ tsp	chopped fresh parsley	2 mL
2	cans (7 oz/198 g) salmon or tuna, drained and mashed	2
6	lasagne noodles, cooked	6
1 cup	ricotta cheese	250 mL
2 cups	mozzarella cheese, freshly grated	500 mL
½ cup	Parmesan cheese, freshly grated	125 mL

1. In a large frying pan, heat the olive oil. Sauté the onion and garlic in the oil. Add the tomatoes, tomato sauce or spaghetti sauce, and herbs. Mix well and simmer slowly until thick. Add the mashed fish and mix thoroughly.

2. Preheat oven to 350° F (180° C).

3. Spread a bit of the sauce over the bottom of a greased 13 x 9-inch (3.5 L) baking dish. Top with ½ the cooked noodles, ½ the sauce, ½ the ricotta cheese and ½ the mozzarella cheese. Repeat once. Sprinkle with the Parmesan cheese. Bake for approximately 30 minutes or until hot and bubbly. Remove from oven and let stand for 10 minutes before serving.

Makes 4 servings.

Scallops in Cheese Sauce

The main season for scallops is from March to November. They are caught in nets dragged along the ocean floor.

2 cups	Cheese Sauce (see page 137)	500 mL
4 tsp	butter	20 mL
2 lb	medium sea scallops (20-30 size)	1 kg
½ cup	Parmesan cheese, freshly grated	125 mL

1. Make the Cheese Sauce in a saucepan, cover and keep warm over hot water.

2. In another saucepan, melt the butter and add the scallops. Cook over medium heat for 2 to 3 minutes. Remove the scallops from the pan and add to the Cheese Sauce. Pour into an earthenware dish and sprinkle with Parmesan cheese. Brown under the broiler.

Makes 4 servings.

Baldrick's Tips

The secret to cooking scallops correctly is to keep turning them in the pan.

Scallops in Garlic Butter

Unlike other bivalves, scallops cannot close their shells tightly.

4 tsp	butter	20 mL
2	cloves garlic, chopped	2
½ cup	mushrooms, sliced	125 mL
2 lb	medium sea scallops (20-30 size)	1 kg
1 cup	chopped tomatoes	250 mL
½ cup	sherry	125 mL
	Salt and pepper	

1. In a frying pan, melt the butter. Add the garlic, mush-rooms and scallops. Cook over medium heat for 3 to 4 minutes. Stir in tomatoes and sherry. Season with salt and pepper to taste and cook for a further 1 to 2 minutes.

Makes 4 servings.

Variation:

Shrimp in Garlic Butter

Substitute 2 lb (1 kg) peeled and deveined shrimp for scallops.

Scallops Provençale

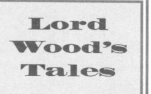

Lord Wood's Tales

A bivalve named for a patron saint – strange, but true. The shell of a Mediterranean scallop was worn by pilgrims to show that they had visited the shrine of St. James at Compostella. There are more than 200 varieties of this cream-colored, coin-shaped mollusk worldwide. But to make it simple, you need to know about only two in North America: the small bay scallop and the large sea scallop.

4 tsp	butter	20 mL
2 lb	medium sea scallops (20-30 size)	1 kg
½ cup	chopped onions	125 mL
2	cloves garlic, crushed and chopped	2
½ cup	white wine	125 mL
2 cups	chopped tomatoes	500 mL
1 cup	tomato sauce	250 mL
	Salt and pepper	
Pinch	chopped fresh parsley	Pinch
	Cooked white rice	

1. In a saucepan, melt the butter. Add the scallops and cook over medium heat for 2 to 3 minutes. Remove the scallops from the pan and set aside. Add the onion and garlic and cook for 1 minute until soft but not brown. Pour off the butter, add the wine and chopped tomatoes, and cook slowly for 4 to 5 minutes. Add the tomato sauce and bring to a boil. Season with salt and pepper to taste. Add the parsley and the scallops. Bring back to a boil.

2. Serve on a bed of white rice.

Makes 4 servings.

Sea Bass Baked in Foil

Lord Wood's Tales

Sea bass is one of the best fish for a novice cook to prepare. It is virtually impossible to ruin it. This fish, which can weigh from 1 to 3 pounds (500 g to 1.5 kg) when fully grown, is popular fare in Italian and Chinese restaurants. A number of fish have numerous names and the sea bass is no exception. It is also known as the sea wolf, sea dance, black bass and striped bass.

1	12 to 16 oz (400 g to 500 g) sea bass, cleaned	1
3	lemon wedges	3
3	lime wedges	3
	Fresh parsley, dill, oregano	
⅓ cup	white wine	75 mL
2 tsp	lemon juice	10 mL
2 tsp	lime juice	10 mL
	Salt and pepper	

1. Score the fish three times on each side. Place a wedge of lemon or lime into each slash. Place the fish in the middle of a large piece of aluminum foil. Stuff the body cavity with a small bunch of fresh herbs. Fold the ends of the aluminum up toward the fish and then fold the sides toward the middle, leaving the top open. Combine the wine and juices and pour over the fish. Season to taste. Close the top of the foil envelope, pinching tightly to make sure it is airtight.

2. Bake in a 350° F (180° C) oven, or barbecue in a closed barbecue, for 25 to 30 minutes.

Makes 2 servings.

Baldrick's Tips

Open the foil pouch at the table. Part of the joy of this dish is the wonderful aromas that come pouring out of the foil envelope when it's opened.

Seafood Crêpes

Lord Wood's Tales

Pancakes are a great way to serve many foods. The Mexicans make the tortilla, the Indians the chapatti and the English the humble pancake. The French have given us crêpes and some wonderful dishes to go with them. Two of my favorite crêpe dishes are seafood crêpes and crêpes Suzette.

Crêpe Batter

2	eggs	2
1 cup	milk	250 mL
1 cup	sifted all-purpose flour	250 mL
¼ tsp	salt	1 mL
¼ cup	vegetable oil	50 mL

1. Beat the eggs in a bowl. Beat in the milk.

2. Combine the flour and salt in another bowl. Make a well in the middle of the dry ingredients and pour in the liquid ingredients. Beat quickly until smooth. Strain if there are any lumps.

3. Heat a crêpe pan or omelet pan. Add vegetable oil and heat until the oil is smoking. Pour off the oil into a dish and save it. Return the pan to the heat and pour in enough batter to cover the pan. Cook over moderate heat for 15 to 20 seconds, flipping when golden brown underneath. Cook the other side for 15 to 20 seconds and turn out onto a plate. Repeat the process using the saved oil until you have used all the batter. Any crêpes that are not used can be stored in the freezer.

Seafood Filling

¼ cup	butter	50 mL
4	green onions, chopped	4
2	sweet green peppers, diced	2
1 cup	sliced mushrooms	250 mL
1 cup	crab meat	250 mL
1 cup	salad shrimp	250 mL
½ cup	Basic White Sauce (page 135)	125 mL

1. In a saucepan, melt the butter. Sauté the green onions, green pepper and mushrooms in the butter until soft. Drain off the butter and add the crab meat and salad shrimp. Mix together and add the Basic White Sauce. Stir over medium heat until thoroughly heated. Remove from heat.

2. Divide the filling among 4 crêpes. Fold the crêpes over and place on a baking sheet. Heat in a 350° F (180° C) oven for 10 minutes and serve.

Makes 4 crêpes.

Baldrick's Tips

The art of creating a good crêpe is to have your pan very hot and the batter paper thin.

Seafood Quiche

Lord Wood's Tales

I was at a restaurant show a couple of years ago and the chappie I was with used that hackneyed expression "Real men don't eat quiche" to a charming young woman serving quiche. She cleverly retaliated with "Real men eat anything they want." He left the booth as fast as his feet could carry him.

The Germans and French both claim this savory custard tart as their own. The British call it Ham and Cheese Pie. They serve it for breakfast, lunch or dinner; even as a midnight snack.

1 cup	milk	250 mL
2	large eggs, beaten	2
	Salt and pepper	
2 tsp	butter	10 mL
6 oz	bay scallops	175 g
6 oz	salad shrimp	175 g
6 oz	snow crab meat	175 g
6 oz	smoked salmon, diced	175 g
1	prebaked 10-inch (25-cm) quiche or pie shell	1
½ cup	grated Edam cheese	125 mL
½ cup	grated old cheddar cheese	125 mL
¼ cup	grated Parmesan cheese	50 mL
1	tomato, sliced	1
1	sweet green pepper, sliced in rings	1

1. Preheat oven to 350° F (180° C).

2. In a saucepan, warm the milk and remove from heat. Add the well-beaten eggs. Season with salt and pepper to taste and mix thoroughly.

3. In another saucepan, melt the butter and sauté the scallops for 2 minutes. Drain off the butter and add the salad shrimp, snow crab meat and smoked salmon. Mix together well. Cover the bottom of the pie shell evenly with the seafood mixture. Pour the milk mixture over the seafood.

4. In a bowl, combine the cheeses and sprinkle over the top of the quiche. Decorate the top with the sliced tomato and green pepper. Bake for 25 to 30 minutes or until a knife inserted into the center comes out clean. Let stand for 5 minutes before serving.

Makes 4 to 6 servings.

Baldrick's Tips

Seafood Quiche tartlets make a wonderful cocktail nibble. We serve them at many of our outside catering functions and they are always the first to go.

Lemon and Lime Marinated Shark Steak

Lord Wood's Tales

The shark is sometimes used in England for fish and chips and in Asian countries for soup. It's not as popular in North America, where it is sometimes served by unscrupulous restaurateurs as swordfish. Shark meat can be tough and should be marinated before grilling or barbecuing.

Lemon and Lime Marinade

1 cup	olive oil	250 mL
½ cup	fresh lemon juice	125 mL
½ cup	fresh lime juice	125 mL
1 tbsp	horseradish, grated or prepared	15 mL
1 tsp	fresh basil, chopped	5 mL
Pinch	dried oregano	Pinch
	Grated rind of 1 lemon and 1 lime	
	Salt and pepper to taste	
4	10-oz (300-g) shark steaks	4

1. **Lemon and Lime Marinade:** In a large dish, combine the marinade ingredients.

2. Put the steaks in the marinade and refrigerate for 24 hours, turning at least once.

3. Preheat broiler.

4. Place the steaks on an oiled baking sheet and grill for 5 to 6 minutes on each side. Baste regularly with the marinade.

Makes 4 servings.

Baldrick's Tips

Use a good quality bristle brush for basting and brushing foods; nylon will melt when it comes in contact with heat and will ruin your creation.

Cajun Shrimp

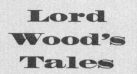

Cajuns are Louisianians descended from French-speaking immigrants from Acadia. Their culture combined with the Creole culture has produced wonderful music, architecture and, of course, food. It's well worth a trip to New Orleans to experience it. In the meantime, try this Cajun Shrimp recipe.

4 tsp	butter	20 mL
2	cloves garlic, finely chopped	2
¼ cup	Cajun seasoning	50 mL
2 lb	medium shrimp (26-30 size), shelled and deveined	1 kg

½	onion, thinly sliced	½
½	sweet green pepper, thinly sliced	½
½	sweet red pepper, thinly sliced	½
1½ cups	whipping cream	375 mL
6 to 8	drops Tabasco sauce	6 to 8
	Orange, lemon and lime wedges	

1. In a saucepan, melt the butter. Add the garlic, Cajun seasoning and shrimp and sauté for about 2 minutes. Remove the shrimp from the pan and set aside. Add the sliced onion, green pepper and red pepper and cook until soft. Stir in the cream and bring to a boil. Add the Tabasco sauce (more if you like it hot) and return the shrimp to the sauce. Bring to a boil again and remove from heat.

2. To serve, garnish with citrus fruit wedges.

Makes 4 servings.

Baldrick's Tips

If you find Cajun seasonings and sauces too hot for your palate, serve citrus fruit alongside to help cool you down.

Deep-Fried Shrimp

**Lord
Wood's
Tales**

You will notice that a Basic Beer Batter is used in this dish. Unfortunately, we have to make this recipe when Baldrick isn't around as our beer tends to run out when he's in the restaurant. I'm sure it isn't going to be long before one of our breweries presents him with an award for his service and dedication to the brewing industry.

2 lb	medium tiger (26-30 size) or large American white (13-15 size) shrimp	1 kg
	All-purpose flour seasoned with salt and pepper	
	Vegetable oil for deep-frying	
1	batch Basic Beer Batter (page 75)	1

1. Shell and devein the shrimp, leaving the tails on. Dip into the seasoned flour, shake off excess and place on a plate.

2. Preheat the oil in the deep fryer to 375° F (190° C). It must be this hot to set the batter and prevent it from becoming oil saturated. Dip the shrimp one at a time in the batter. Place, rather than drop, the shrimp in the hot oil. Dropping the shrimp might cause the oil to splatter, burning you. Stir the shrimp after 1 minute and let cook for another 2½ to 3 minutes until golden brown and crispy. Remove from the oil and drain well.

3. Serve with Spicy Cocktail Sauce (page 141).

Makes 4 servings.

Baldrick's Tips

When deep-frying, don't fry too many shrimp at one time; the temperature of the oil will drop and the shrimp will become soggy.

Skate with Black Butter

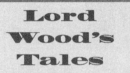

Skate is a very tasty, unappreciated fish, one of our favorites. The only parts of this deep sea flat fish that are used are the wings. "Wings" is the term used by "fish people" to describe the sides of the skate's main body.

4	8-oz (250-g) skate wings, cleaned	4
¼ cup	vegetable oil	50 mL
	All-purpose flour seasoned with salt and pepper	
¼ cup	butter	50 mL
4 tsp	malt vinegar	20 mL
2 tbsp	very small capers	25 mL
	Chopped fresh parsley	

1. Wash the skate wings and dry on paper towels.

2. In a large frying pan, heat the oil. Dip the skate wings into the seasoned flour and pat lightly to remove any excess flour. Place the skate in the hot oil and cook over medium heat for 5 to 6 minutes on each side, or longer if the wings are thick. Remove from the pan and dry on paper towels.

3. Drain the oil from the frying pan and add the butter. Cook until well browned, almost black. Stir the vinegar into the butter.

4. To serve, arrange the skate on a serving plate. Pour the blackened butter over the fish and garnish with the capers and chopped parsley.

Makes 4 servings.

Baldrick's Tips

S kate must be fresh. If it's past its prime, it will smell like ammonia.

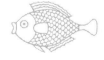

Jerk Snapper

Lord Wood's Tales

Jerk! Where we come from it's a way of describing someone who does not always agree with our opinions or recipes. It is, in fact, a West Indian way of cooking. Try our Jerk Marinade on porgy, parrot fish and shrimp, as well as on snapper. It can also be used on chicken, beef or pork.

Jerk Marinade

1	onion, finely chopped	1
½ cup	chopped green onions	125 mL
1	hot red pepper, finely chopped	1
3 tbsp	soya sauce	50 mL
1 tbsp	vegetable oil	15 mL
1 tbsp	white vinegar	15 mL
2 tsp	sugar	10 mL
1 tsp	allspice	5 mL
1 tsp	salt	5 mL
1 tsp	ground black pepper	5 mL
½ tsp	ground nutmeg	2 mL
½ tsp	ground cinnamon	2 mL
2	1-lb (500-g) snappers	2

1. *Jerk Marinade:* Blend all the ingredients together in a food processor or blender until the marinade has a paste-like consistency.

2. One hour before cooking the fish, rub the marinade into the snappers.

3. Place the fish in a greased baking dish. Bake in the oven at 350° F (180° C) for approximately 25 minutes. The fish will be done when it flakes easily with a fork.

Makes 4 servings.

Baldrick's Tips

To spice up the marinade even more, add a few drops of Tabasco sauce.

Sole Veronique

Sole is associated with quality and delicate flavor. Dover, lemon, gray, plaice and yellowtail are a few of the many different types. In fact, "sole" has become a popular term to describe many types of flat fish. However, many are not sole but flounder. Sole is less rounded than flounder and is thicker.

2 cups	Court Bouillon (page 59)	500 mL
4	8-oz (250-g) sole fillets	4
	Fish Velouté (page 139)	
1 cup	seedless green and black grapes	250 mL

1. In a large saucepan, bring the Court Bouillon to a boil.

2. Roll the fillets and add to the Court Bouillon. Return to the boil. Immediately reduce the heat so that the liquid is just simmering, not boiling. Cook for approximately 5 minutes. Lift the fillets carefully from the liquid and drain well. Place on a baking sheet, coat with Fish Velouté and glaze under the broiler.

3. To serve, place on a serving plate and garnish with grapes.

Makes 4 servings.

Baldrick's Tips

Always end a good meal with good coffee or good tea.

Sole Stuffed with Crab and Shrimp

Lord Wood's Tales

Sole Stuffed with Crab and Shrimp, not to mention a hint of wine, is a special dish for that special occasion — an excellent entrée for making an impression on the boss or, in our case, the publisher.

4	8-oz (250-g) lemon sole fillets	4
8 oz	Alaskan crab meat	250 g
8 oz	salad shrimp	250 g
1 tbsp	finely chopped onion	15 mL
½ cup	Basic Fish Stock (page 60)	125 mL
¼ cup	dry white wine	50 mL
	Juice of ½ lemon	
1 tbsp	soft butter	15 mL
1 tbsp	all-purpose flour	15 mL
¼ cup	whipping cream	50 mL
4	Lemon wedges	4
	Fresh parsley sprigs	

1. Skin the sole fillets, wash and place on work surface skinned side up.

2. In a bowl, combine the crab meat and salad shrimp. Divide into 4 equal parts and place a portion on each sole fillet. Roll up the fillet, enclosing the crab and shrimp mixture completely. Place in a buttered earthenware dish, sprinkle with the onion and add the Fish

Stock. Cover the fish with buttered parchment paper or aluminum foil. Cook gently at 350° F (180° C) for 10 minutes. Remove from oven, place the fish on a serving plate and keep warm.

3. Pour the stock into a saucepan and add the wine and lemon juice. Bring to a boil. In a bowl, make beurre manié by rubbing together the butter and the flour as for pastry. Form into small balls and drop into the hot liquid to thicken it. Stir well. Strain into a clean saucepan and bring to a boil again. Whisk in the whipping cream; heat but do not boil.

4. To serve, coat the sole fillets with the sauce and garnish with lemon wedges and parsley sprigs.

Makes 4 servings.

Sole Bonne Femme

Lord Wood's Tales

Dover sole got its name from the port in England where it was first landed. If it's not from England or France, it's not Dover sole. Because of the high cost of Dover sole, we recommend substituting lemon sole if you're serving this fish with a sauce.

AWFUL! Sh, cook for 20 minutes. Also, use whipping cream, not coffee cream! *Fish Schtick* Betterget, fry it!!

4	8-oz (250-g) lemon sole fillets	4
1 cup	finely chopped mushrooms	250 mL
½ cup	finely chopped onion	125 mL
2 tbsp	chopped fresh parsley	25 mL
1 cup	white wine	250 mL
½ cup	whipping cream	125 mL
4 tsp	butter	20 mL

1. Roll the sole fillets and place in a greased ovenproof dish. Top with the mushrooms, onion and parsley. Add the white wine and cover. Cook in a 350° F (180° C) oven for 10 to 12 minutes. Remove fish, drain, reserving liquid, and keep warm on a serving plate.

2. Pour the cooking liquid into a saucepan and bring to a boil. Add the cream and return to a boil, stirring constantly. Remove from heat and add the butter. Stir until the butter is melted.

3. To serve, pour the sauce over the fillet.

Makes 4 servings.

Baldrick's Tips

To keep mushrooms white, dip them in a mixture of lemon juice and water.

Goujons of Sole

Lord Wood's Tales

Goujons of sole served with Tartare Sauce (page 142) or Spicy Cocktail Sauce (page 141) are an excellent lunch. These tasty little morsels are the grown-up version of fish fingers. Down south they tend to use grouper, but in Europe they use sole and a nicer-sounding name – "goujon" rather than "the finger."

2 lb	sole fillets	1 kg

Basic Bread Coating

2	eggs	2
1 cup	milk	250 mL
1 cup	all-purpose flour seasoned with salt and pepper	250 mL
2 cups	dry bread crumbs	500 mL

1. Place the sole fillets on a cutting board and cut diagonally into strips that are ¼ inch (.5 cm) wide and between 1¼ inch (3 cm) and 1¾ inch (4.5 cm) long.

2. ***Basic Bread Coating:*** Whisk the eggs and milk together in a bowl. Put the flour in a second bowl and the bread crumbs in a third bowl. Place the 3 bowls in the order of the breading sequence: flour to the left, milk and egg mixture in the middle and bread crumbs to the right.

3. Dip each piece of fish in the flour, ensuring that it is completely "dusted." Shake off any excess flour and dip in the milk and egg mixture. Coat thoroughly and lift out, allowing any excess liquid to drain off. Roll in the bread crumbs. Lift out and roll between the palms of your hands to ensure an even coating and to remove any excess crumbs.

4. To cook, follow the deep-frying method on page 116.

Makes 4 servings.

Baldrick's Tips

The Basic Bread Coating can be used to coat many types of food for deep-frying, including breaded mushrooms and zucchini — poor man's scampi!

Blackened Swordfish

We use our own Cajun seasoning on swordfish and many other types of fish. I am pleased to say that it has been often imitated but never bettered. Blackened fish is prepared using a cooking method that originated in the southern United States. It doesn't have a chili, curry, garlic or jerk flavor, but its own unique taste.

4	8-oz (250-g) swordfish steaks	4
2 tbsp	melted butter	25 mL
¼ cup	Cajun seasoning	50 mL

1. Heat a skillet until it is extremely hot. Wash the swordfish steak and pat dry with paper towels. Brush generously with the melted butter and coat with Cajun seasoning. Make sure the steak is well coated with seasoning. Place the fish in the hot skillet and reduce heat to medium. Cook for 3 to 4 minutes each side. When turning the fish and removing it from the pan, be careful not to knock off the seasoning.

Makes 4 servings.

Trout Almondine

Lord Wood's Tales

Trout, like salmon, can be wild or farm-raised. We have had great success working with the Ontario Trout Farmers' Association and Foodland Ontario. Poached, pan-fried, stuffed, baked or smoked, trout is a prince among freshwater fish.

4	8-oz (250-g) rainbow trout, butterflied	4
½ cup	vegetable oil	125 mL
	All-purpose flour seasoned with salt and pepper	
1 cup	sliced almonds	250 mL
	Chopped fresh parsley	
	Lemon slices	

1. Wash the trout and pat dry with paper towels. Heat the oil in a large frying pan. Dip the trout into seasoned flour to coat and shake off excess flour. Place the fish into the hot oil, skin side up. Reduce the heat to medium and cook each side for 2½ minutes. Lift the fish from the oil and drain well. Place on a serving plate and keep warm.

2. Sprinkle the almond slices on a baking sheet and toast under the broiler. Watch them carefully, because they burn easily.

3. To serve, sprinkle the almonds over the trout and garnish with chopped parsley and lemon slices.

Makes 4 servings.

Baldrick's Tips

To barbecue trout, make use of those outside lettuce leaves. Season the trout with a little dill or thyme and salt and pepper. Wrap the washed lettuce leaves around the fish and tie with string. Cook on the barbecue for about 7 minutes each side until the lettuce is brown, turning periodically. Remove the string and lettuce, and serve.

Bacchus Whitefish

Lord Wood's Tales

Bacchus is the Greek god of wine, hence Bacchus Whitefish. Although the whitefish is a member of the salmon family, its flesh, as its name suggests, is white rather than pink. Other names for whitefish are cisco, chub and tullibee. This delicate-tasting, great Canadian fish is very popular and when just caught and cooked, puts fish lovers in their element.

1 cup	seedless green grapes	250 mL
1 cup	seedless black grapes	250 mL
4	8-oz (250-g) whitefish fillets	4
	Salt and pepper	
1 cup	dry white wine	250 mL
1 cup	water	250 mL

1. Wash the grapes and cut in half. Put them in the bottom of an ovenproof dish, place the whitefish on top and season with salt and pepper to taste. Combine the wine and water and add to the dish. Bake, covered, in a 350° F (180° C) oven for 10 to 12 minutes, basting the fish twice during the cooking time.

2. To serve, place the cooked fish on a serving plate and cover with cooking liquid and grapes.

Makes 4 servings.

Red Herring (Crème Caramel)

Lord Wood's Tales

Why have we put a recipe for Crème Caramel in a fish cookbook? Well, we decided to give you a break from fish recipes and we wanted to see if you had been paying attention. Seriously, we both like this dessert and find it a refreshing treat after eating fish. It's easy to make and you can add a little almond liqueur to the milk to make it even more special.

Caramel

½ cup	water	125 mL
½ cup	sugar	125 mL

Custard

2 cups	milk	500 mL
4	eggs, beaten	4
¼ cup	sugar	50 mL
3 or 4 drops	vanilla extract	3 or 4 drops

Whipped cream (optional)

1. **Caramel:** Put about ¾ of the water in a thick-bottomed saucepan and add the sugar. Bring gently to a boil and boil until the liquid turns golden brown. Remove from heat and add the remaining water to the caramel mixture. Return to heat and reboil until the caramel mixture and water blend together. Pour into 4 custard cups, coating the bottom of each cup.

2. Preheat oven to 350° F (180° C).

3. *Custard:* In a saucepan, warm the milk. Add the beaten eggs, sugar and vanilla and stir. Strain and pour over the caramel leaving 1/4 inch (.5 cm) at the top of each cup. Place the cups in an ovenproof dish. Fill the dish with water to the halfway mark on the cups. Bake for approximately 30 minutes or until set. Remove the custard cups from the dish and allow to cool thoroughly.

4. To serve, loosen the edges with a wet knife and turn out onto a plate. Garnish with whipped cream, if desired.

Makes 4 servings.

Baldrick's Tips

If this book is too hard for you to follow, give up and come eat with us at the Old Fish Market Restaurant.

Butters and Sauces

Butters

Almond Butter

We like this butter on barbecued or broiled red snapper or rainbow trout.

½ cup	butter	125 mL
2 tbsp	ground almonds	25 mL
1 tbsp	lemon juice	15 mL
1 tbsp	lime juice	15 mL
2 or 3 drops	Tabasco sauce	2 or 3 drops

1. In a saucepan, melt the butter. Add the almonds and brown in the butter. Remove from heat and add the remaining ingredients. Mix well and pour over fish.

   Makes about ½ cup (125 mL).

Anchovy Butter

½ cup	soft butter	125 mL
2 tsp	anchovy paste	10 mL
	or	
2	anchovy fillets, chopped very fine	2
	Salt and pepper, to taste	

1. In a bowl, combine ingredients and mix well. Place the butter in a piece of aluminum foil and shape into a roll. Refrigerate until ready to use.

Makes about ½ cup (125 mL).

Brandy and Walnut Butter

An excellent topping for barbecued fish, especially Atlantic salmon.

½ cup	soft butter	125 mL
2 tbsp	chopped walnuts	25 mL
2 tbsp	brandy	25 mL
	Salt and pepper, to taste	

1. In a bowl, combine ingredients and mix well. Place the butter in a piece of aluminum foil and shape into a roll. Refrigerate until ready to use.

Makes about ½ cup (125 mL).

Dill Butter

A great finish to poached salmon or trout.

½ cup	butter	125 mL
2 tsp	chopped fresh dill	10 mL

1. In a bowl, combine the butter and dill. Place the butter in a piece of aluminum foil and shape into a roll. Refrigerate until ready to use.

Makes about ½ cup (125 mL).

Lemon Butter

½ cup	butter	125 mL
1 tsp	grated lemon rind	5 mL
1 tsp	lemon juice or lime juice	5 mL
1 tsp	chopped fresh parsley	5 mL
1 tsp	mustard (optional)	5 mL
1 tsp	capers (optional)	5 mL

1. In a saucepan, melt the butter and stir in the other ingredients. This butter can be "spiced up" by adding mustard and/or capers. Pour over grilled or baked fish fillets or steaks.

Makes about ½ cup (125 mL).

Parsley Butter

½ cup	soft butter	125 mL
1 tbsp	finely chopped fresh parsley	15 mL
	Juice of ½ lemon	
	Salt and pepper, to taste	

1. In a bowl, combine ingredients and mix well. Place the butter in a piece of aluminum foil and shape into a roll. Refrigerate until ready to use.

Makes about ½ cup (125 mL).

Tarragon Butter

This is great for adding a little "pep" to mild fish like cod, orange roughy or sole.

| ½ cup | soft butter | 125 mL |
| 1 tbsp | dried tarragon | 15 mL |

1. In a bowl, combine ingredients and mix well. Place the butter in a piece of aluminum foil and shape into a roll. Refrigerate until ready to use.

Makes about ½ cup (125 mL).

Sauces

Basic White Sauce

¼ cup	butter	50 mL
¼ cup	all-purpose flour	50 mL
2 cups	milk, warmed	500 mL

1. In a heavy saucepan, melt the butter. Stir in the flour and cook over low heat for 2 minutes without coloring. Gradually add the warm milk and whisk until smooth and thickened. Strain if necessary.

Makes 2 cups (500 mL).

Variations:

Cream Sauce

Add ¼ cup (50 mL) whipping cream.

Dill Sauce

Add 3 to 4 tsp (15 to 20 mL) dill weed.

Egg Sauce

Add 2 hard-cooked eggs, diced.

Mustard Sauce

Add 2 to 3 tsp (10 to 15 mL) prepared English mustard. This is a particularly good sauce to use on a grilled oily fish like herring.

Parsley Sauce

Add 3 to 4 tsp (15 to 20 mL) chopped fresh parsley.

Béarnaise Sauce

2 tbsp	finely chopped onions	25 mL
2 tbsp	malt vinegar	25 mL
2 tsp	dried tarragon	10 mL
5	peppercorns, crushed	5
4	egg yolks	4
	Juice from 1 lemon, warmed	
1 cup	melted butter	250 mL
Pinch	dried tarragon	Pinch

1. In a saucepan, simmer the first four ingredients until the liquid is reduced by half. Strain into a mixing bowl and allow to cool. Set the bowl over, not in, a saucepan of boiling water. Add the egg yolks and whisk until the sauce starts to thicken. Add the lemon juice and mix well. Remove from heat and gradually add the melted butter, beating until the sauce thickens. Add a pinch of dried tarragon.

Makes about 1 cup (250 mL).

Cheese Sauce

3 tbsp	butter	50 mL
3 tbsp	all-purpose flour	50 mL
1½ cups	milk	375 mL
	Salt and pepper	
1 cup	grated cheddar cheese	250 mL

1. In a small saucepan, melt the butter over medium heat. Blend in flour for 1 to 2 minutes. Gradually stir in the milk and continue stirring until the mixture thickens. Season with salt and pepper to taste. Quickly stir in the cheese until it melts and immediately remove from heat.

Makes about 2 cups (500 mL).

Curry Sauce

¼ cup	butter	50 mL
1 tbsp	finely chopped onion	15 mL
1	small clove garlic, crushed and chopped	1
2 tbsp	all-purpose flour	25 mL
2 tbsp	medium Madras curry powder	25 mL
1 tbsp	tomato paste	15 mL
2 cups	chicken stock	500 mL
½ cup	plain yogurt	125 mL
1 tbsp	mango chutney	15 mL
1 tbsp	shredded coconut	15 mL
1 tbsp	sultana raisins	15 mL
2	apples, diced	2
	Pineapple pieces, currants, banana slices, orange segments, almond slices (optional)	

1. In a saucepan, melt the butter. Add the onion and garlic and cook for 2 to 3 minutes until soft but not browned. Stir in the flour and curry powder and cook for 2 to 3 minutes until the mixture is a sandy texture. Mix in the tomato paste and cook for 5 minutes.

2. In another saucepan, bring the stock to a boil. Add to the curry mixture, mix well and bring to a boil. Reduce heat and simmer for 30 minutes. Remove from heat.

3. Stir in yogurt, mango chutney, shredded coconut, sultana raisins and diced apples, as well as optional ingredients, if desired. Refrigerate for 24 to 48 hours before reheating and serving.

Makes about 3 cups (750 mL).

Fish Velouté

2 tbsp	butter	25 mL
2 tbsp	all-purpose flour	25 mL
2 cups	Basic Fish Stock (page 60)	500 mL

1. In a heavy saucepan, melt the butter and stir in the flour. Mix well and cook over moderate heat until the mixture has a sandy texture. Remove from heat and allow to cool for 4 to 5 minutes.

2. In another saucepan, heat the stock. Gradually add the hot stock to the butter mixture and stir until the sauce is smooth. Bring to a boil, reduce heat and simmer for 30 minutes. Strain through a sieve and use as required.

Makes about 2 cups (500 mL) .

Hollandaise Sauce

4	egg yolks	4
	Juice from 1 lemon, warmed	
1 cup	melted butter	250 mL

1. Set a mixing bowl over, not in, a saucepan of boiling
water. Add the egg yolks and whisk until they start to
thicken. Add the warm lemon juice and mix well.
Remove the bowl from the heat and gradually add the
warm melted butter, beating until the sauce thickens.

Makes about 1 cup (250 mL).

Marie Rose Sauce

¼ cup	ketchup	50 mL
2 tbsp	sherry	25 mL
2 or 3 drops	Worcestershire sauce	2 or 3 drops
2 drops	Tabasco sauce	2 drops
1½ cups	Mayonnaise (see next page)	375 mL

1. In a bowl, combine the first 4 ingredients. Add the
Mayonnaise and mix well.

Makes about 2 cups (500 mL).

Mayonnaise

4	egg yolks	4
4 tsp	white vinegar	20 mL
Pinch	dry mustard	Pinch
	Salt and pepper, to taste	
2 cups	olive oil	500 mL
2 tsp	boiling water	10 mL

1. In a mixing bowl, combine the egg yolks, vinegar and seasonings and whisk thoroughly. Slowly pour in the oil, whisking continuously. Stir in the boiling water. Refrigerate until ready to use.

Makes about 2 cups (500 mL).

Spicy Cocktail Sauce

A traditional accompaniment for oysters on the half shell, shrimp cocktails and many breaded and deep-fried seafoods.

1¼ cups	chili sauce	300 mL
¾ cup	ketchup	175 mL
1 to 2 tsp	prepared horseradish sauce	5 to 10 mL
2 or 3 drops	Tabasco sauce	2 or 3 drops

1. In a mixing bowl, combine ingredients. Refrigerate until ready to use.

Makes about 2 cups (500 mL).

Tartare Sauce

Unlike our recipe, many North American tartare sauce recipes call for the use of relish or sweet pickles. We're sure you'll appreciate the difference in flavor that capers and gherkin pickles make.

1½ cups	Mayonnaise (page 141)	375 mL
¼ cup	finely chopped sour gherkin pickles	50 mL
2 tbsp	finely chopped onion	25 mL
2 tbsp	finely chopped capers	25 mL
2 tbsp	chopped fresh parsley	25 mL

1. In a mixing bowl, combine ingredients. Refrigerate until ready to use.

Makes about 2 cups (500 mL).

About the Authors

Christopher ("Baldrick") McNulty, corporate chef of the Old Fish Market Restaurants Ltd., was born in Dartford, England. Although thought at an early age to be Dartford's long-lost son, Baldrick was displaced by another famous personality. The ageless rock star Mick Jagger, who also hails from Dartford, became the new light of Dartford's eye and Baldrick was forced to look for bigger fish to fry.

As a young boy, Baldrick formed an early affection for fish and to this day counts them among his best friends. After finishing his chef's apprenticeship, he worked for many fine establishments in and around the London area. Hearing that Canada might be the original fish mecca of the world, Baldrick then decided to grace our great country with his presence and wealth of fishy knowledge. Today he continues his love affair with fish at the Old Fish Market and declares that he has found happiness beyond his wildest dreams.

John ("My Lord") Wood, co-owner of the Old Fish Market Restaurants, was also born in jolly old England. Like another bygone hero, Robin Hood, John came from Sherwood Forest. However, unlike Robin Hood, who was well known for his penchant for stealing from the rich and giving to the poor, John never quite grasped that concept. He decidedly wanted to join the ranks of the rich and set about planning his future.

Early in life, John discovered that good food and drink gave him an immense amount of pleasure. Then he found out that if he joined a brewery, he could learn to cook at their expense. This he did. Working his way up to manager in a variety of companies, hotels and hostelries, John soon found that instead of taking orders he'd much rather give them. After owning a number of restaurants and after a number of financial follies, the jolly old taxman of jolly old England inserted himself into John's business affairs. My Lord John was forced to pay up and soon fled his homeland to become, with his friend and partner, the proud co-owner of the Old Fish Market Restaurants in Toronto, Windsor and Ottawa. After a misadventure in the Florida market, where the weather and good citizens of Miami were just too darn hot to put up with John and his daft fish, he prudently returned to Canada with his fish stories, strange accent and wealth of fish knowledge, which he will share with you if you ask (and even if you don't).

Index

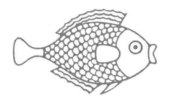

*W*ell, that's that. If you got this far, you deserve a medal or at least an excellent fish meal, which is why we've enclosed this Gift Certificate for your use at any of our restaurants. (Food only, as the liquor police won't let us buy you a beverage.) Now just think of all the unfortunate readers who did not take the trouble to complete this book and cannot take advantage of this offer — don't tell them and we might make some money this year!

We hope you found this book enjoyable and informative. Remember: don't be afraid, go for it, grab your fish by the horns (mixed metaphor) and experiment.

There are so many people to thank for their assistance in producing *Fish Schtick*, we cannot begin to try. Next time you could be one of them; write in and let us know how you got on. We love our fishy world and are always on the lookout for ideas and great but simple recipes. Write to:

John Wood/Chris McNulty
c/o Doubleday Canada Limited
105 Bond Street
Toronto, Ontario
M5B 1Y3
Canada

Thanks,

John Wood

P.S. What about the book cover, eh?

152